Preface

The *Report on the World Social Situation, 2003* is the sixteenth in a series of reports on the subject dating back to 1952. Over the years, the report has served as a background document for discussion and policy analysis of socio-economic matters at the intergovernmental level. In addition, the *Report* has aimed at contributing to the identification of emerging social trends of international concern and to the analysis of relationships among major development issues that have both international and national dimensions.

In its resolution 56/177 of 19 December 2001, the General Assembly requested the Secretary-General to change the periodicity of the *Report on the World Social Situation* from a four-year cycle to a two-year cycle. The present *Report* is the first produced on a biennial basis. That is not, however, the only change to the *Report*. Its content should be seen as part of the new initiatives put forward by the Secretary-General in his quest to renew the capacity of the Organization to provide a space for genuine dialogue and serve as a catalyst for effective action.

The 2003 *Report* has two new main features. First, it takes a thematic approach, addressing one priority theme in depth: the issue of social vulnerability. The objective of the *Report* is to develop a frame of reference for identifying the sources of social vulnerabilities and explore strategies to reduce the vulnerabilities of selected social groups. The second new feature of the 2003 *Report* is an attempt to increase its policy relevance by putting forward explicit policy recommendations. Every effort has been made to address the issue of social vulnerability in a concise way, making the *Report* a more readable, shorter and better focused document.

The *Report* was prepared by the Division for Social Policy and Development of the Department of Economic and Social Affairs of the United Nations Secretariat.

Contents

Explanatory notes

The designations employed and the presentation of the material in this publication do not imply the expression of any opinion whatsoever on the part of the Secretariat of the United Nations concerning the legal status of any country or territory or of its authorities, or concerning the delimitations of its frontiers.

The term "country" as used in the text of the present report also refers, as appropriate, to territories or areas.

Mention of the names of firms and commercial products does not imply the endorsement of the United Nations.

Reference to dollars ($) indicates United States dollars, unless otherwise stated.

When a print edition of a source exists, the print version is the authoritative one. United Nations documents reproduced online are deemed official only as they appear in the United Nations Official Document System. United Nations documentation obtained from other United Nations and non-United Nations sources is for informational purposes only. The Organization does not make any warranties or representations as to the accuracy or completeness of such materials.

Unless otherwise indicated, the country classification set out below has been used:

Developed market economies:

North America (excluding Mexico), Southern and Western Europe (excluding Cyprus, Malta and former Yugoslavia), Australia, Japan, New Zealand.

Economies in transition:

Albania, Bulgaria, Czech Republic, Hungary, Poland, Romania, Slovakia and the former USSR, comprising the Baltic Republics and the member countries of the Commonwealth of Independent States (CIS).

Developing countries:

Latin America and the Caribbean, Africa, Asia and the Pacific (excluding Australia, Japan and New Zealand), Cyprus, Malta, former Yugoslavia.

Least developed countries (49 countries):

Afghanistan, Angola, Bangladesh, Benin, Bhutan, Burkina Faso, Burundi, Cambodia, Cape Verde, Central African Republic, Chad, Comoros, Democratic Republic of the Congo (formerly Zaire), Djibouti, Equatorial Guinea, Eritrea, Ethiopia, Gambia, Guinea, Guinea-Bissau, Haiti, Kiribati, Lao People's Democratic Republic, Lesotho, Liberia, Madagascar, Malawi, Maldives, Mali, Mauritania, Mozambique, Myanmar, Nepal, Niger, Rwanda, Samoa, Sao Tome and Principe, Senegal, Sierra Leone, Solomon Islands, Somalia, Sudan, Togo, Tuvalu, Uganda, United Republic of Tanzania, Vanuatu, Yemen, Zambia.

The designations of country groups in the text and the tables are intended solely for statistical or analytical convenience and do not necessarily express a judgement about the stage reached by a particular country or area in the development process.

The following abbreviations have been used:

FDI	foreign direct investment
HIV/AIDS	human immunodeficiency virus/acquired immunodeficiency syndrome
ILO	International Labour Organization
NEPAD	New Partnership for Africa's Development
OECD	Organisation for Economic Cooperation and Development
PRSP	Poverty Reduction Strategy Paper
TRIPS	Agreement on Trade-related Aspects of Intellectual Property Rights
UNAIDS	Joint United Nations Programme on HIV/AIDS
UNDP	United Nations Development Programme
UNESCO	United Nations Educational, Scientific and Cultural Organization
UNHCR	Office of the United Nations High Commissioner for Refugees
UNICEF	United Nations Children's Fund
UNRWA	United Nations Relief and Works Agency for Palestine Refugees in the Near East
WHO	World Health Organization
WIPO	World Intellectual Property Organization
WTO	World Trade Organization

Executive summary

1.   No social group is inherently vulnerable. However, all groups face vulnerabilities that are largely the outcome of economic, social and cultural barriers that restrict opportunities for and impede the social integration and participation of the members of the group. Common to the analysis of vulnerabilities among the different groups is the existence of some form of exclusion that is not primarily market related or market generated but socially generated. The main emphasis in the present report is therefore on group-specific vulnerabilities and, consequently, on the challenges of social inclusion. That approach helps to identify barriers that prevent social integration for the groups. The particular groups dealt with in the *Report* include children and youth; older persons; persons with disabilities; indigenous persons; migrants; and persons in situations of conflict, with due consideration for gender-specific challenges.

2.   Vulnerability and poverty interact with each other, creating a vicious circle in which the two reinforce each other. Poor people are the most vulnerable to economic shocks, material losses and losses of well-being. Such events can easily destroy the ability of the poor to move out of poverty, both in the long run and in the short run, by depleting their human and physical assets, a process that may be irreversible. An increase in vulnerability especially affects the poor because they have greater exposure to many downward risks (such as illness, death, loss of employment or famine), and they are less capable of coping with them. Poverty and inequalities also may increase vulnerability indirectly by fuelling social tensions and undermining the social cohesion needed to pre-empt and respond to emerging dangers.

3.   While vulnerability, uncertainty and insecurity are not new in people's lives, what is new is that the causes and manifestations of those elements have multiplied and changed profoundly over the last decade. Examples include civil strife and the proliferation of conflicts; growing inequalities within and among countries, further accentuated by globalization; mixed outcomes of poverty reduction efforts; increased mobility of populations; and changes in family structures.

4.   In order to achieve a reduction in vulnerability, it is important to understand the factors and forces that lie at its source: what makes an individual or group vulnerable, or at a greater risk of becoming vulnerable, to a variety of social ills? Both internal and external dynamics are at play in determining the level of vulnerability, encompassing a variety of economic, social and environmental concerns.

5.   Although income insecurity, including lack of access to gainful employment, stands out as one of the most important sources of vulnerability, it is not only the lack of financial assets and income that reduces coping capacity. Such social ills as poor health, limited access to health services and limited or no access to education are important contributors, and they are significant factors determining earnings capacity and personal development. In addition, the presence and persistence of sociocultural biases and discriminatory attitudes and practices can be readily identified as major contributors to vulnerabilities.

6.   Proper identification of trends and an assessment of the underlying causes leading to structural vulnerabilities can provide a proper basis for well thought out and balanced policy action. Anchoring the policy response to empowerment and social integration increases the chances of success in the long run. It is to those

issues — sources of vulnerability and policy responses to vulnerability — that the present report is devoted.

Policy challenges and recommendations

Addressing barriers to employment

7. Experiences in the last two decades of the twentieth century clearly show that a reorientation of macroeconomic policy to target employment creation explicitly is needed in both industrialized and developing countries in order to reduce poverty and vulnerability in a permanent fashion. The shift in policy focus would be a concrete, practical example of the integration of social and economic policies; it is an approach that is widely embraced. The implementation of employment creation policy is complex: it must meet the challenges presented by various economic sectors and attend to the concerns of diverse social groups, as well as address gender-based discrimination.

8. Trade and diffusion of technology can reinforce economic growth, job creation and productivity gains when appropriate macroeconomic policy that promotes job-creating growth is in place. Appropriate macroeconomic policies should be advanced that result in an increase in productive investment and employment-intensive growth.

9. Industrialized economies should be encouraged to provide greater market access for the exports of goods from developing countries as a means of supporting their development and improving existing labour market conditions in those countries through export growth. Market access for exports by developing countries is not a matter of charity; a number of international agreements (including World Trade Organization agreements) call for the phasing-out of all forms of export subsidies, substantial reductions in trade-distorting domestic support and the improvement of market access for the developing countries.

10. Development policies should be refashioned so as to guard against premature liberalization and misguided policy reforms, which, in the absence of appropriate institutions and productive capacity, can serve to worsen labour-market conditions in developing countries.

11. The problem of youth unemployment should be addressed through a combination of efforts to improve their employability, enhance their job skills and remove legislative and other barriers that can lead to discriminatory practices adversely affecting youth employment.

12. Credit policies should be modified so as to enable older persons, women and young people who wish to start their own businesses to gain access more readily to microcredit and other loan schemes.

13. Older persons should have the opportunity to continue working and contributing to the economy for as long as they wish. To that end, older men and women should be able to avail themselves of retraining and skills-upgrading programmes to help them keep up with technological and other work-based changes.

14. Persons with disabilities in developing countries should be supported in their efforts to integrate more fully into the mainstream economy through wider participation in the labour market. Opportunities for self-employment should be

encouraged, including improved access to credit schemes, along with the provision of training in all aspects of small business operations.

15. In developed countries, it is important to mainstream disabled men and women into open employment rather than place them in sheltered or supported work environments.

Promoting social integration and social protection

16. Discrimination and social or cultural biases will not automatically disappear with a reduction in poverty. Explicit policy measures and strict enforcement of legal protection are needed to address and rectify barriers to social integration.

17. Barriers to social equity and social integration deprive marginalized populations not only of the ability to protect their economic rights and achieve their full potential to contribute to society, but also of the opportunity to earn adequate income. Therefore, policy measures to reduce social vulnerability need to take an integrated approach to the problem while keeping appropriate priorities to maximize the effectiveness of such policy responses.

18. A society for all — girls and boys, men and women — encompasses the goal of providing all social groups with the opportunity to contribute to society. To work towards that goal, it is necessary to remove whatever excludes them or discriminates against them and to enable their full participation in decision-making.

19. With a view towards fostering sustainable livelihoods for people with disabilities, national and international efforts should promote rehabilitation strategies designed to maximize functional capacities of persons with disabilities; architectural and design strategies that remove unnecessary barriers in the environment; and inclusion and empowerment strategies to facilitate greater participation in society.

20. Persons with disabilities should be granted equal opportunities to participate in mainstream education, to seek productive and gainful employment in open labour markets and to have access to appropriate social safety nets in terms of income maintenance and services.

21. As elaborated in the Standard Rules on the Equalization of Opportunities for Persons with Disabilities (General Assembly resolution 48/96, annex), universal design concepts should be advanced to ensure that products and environments are usable by all people to the greatest extent possible. Improving accessibility of persons with disabilities to the physical environment and to information and communication technologies will help them overcome barriers that restrict their access to social and economic opportunities.

22. Using the international human rights instruments as a framework, laws and policies should be formulated and enacted to protect the rights of indigenous peoples and guard them against institutional racism and discrimination. Issues concerning land rights and the protection of indigenous peoples' cultures warrant particular consideration. The full participation of indigenous peoples in the design, implementation and evaluation of those laws and policies should be guaranteed as part of an open dialogue between indigenous peoples and mainstream society.

23. Although as a group, older persons are not inherently vulnerable, the ageing process can force people to adjust to physical, social and economic circumstances

over which they have little control, increasing their level of risk. Older persons' vulnerabilities can be significantly reduced through a combination of their own defences built up over a lifetime and the presence of outside sources of support.

24. Policy makers, including development institutions and national Governments, should pay greater attention to the impact of a growing older population on their development strategies, being mindful of the contributions that older men and women can make to the development process as well as the demands they will place on social protection and care services.

25. As recognized at the Second World Assembly on Ageing in 2002, ageing should be mainstreamed into all policy areas, most notably into national development frameworks and poverty reduction strategies. Furthermore, issues concerning older persons should be addressed within a context of poverty reduction, participation, gender equality and human rights, and linked to development targets and agendas.

26. Given the enormous implications of population ageing, policies that reduce the vulnerability of older persons should be advanced with a view to producing gains not only for older persons and their families, but for the community, society at large and future generations.

27. Community-based targeting of social protection services can offer a promising means of delivering services to those in need, as the community becomes directly involved in identifying beneficiaries, thereby increasing accuracy in determining beneficiaries and promoting equity and inclusion by fostering greater local control over the programmes. Community-based targeting should be advanced in conjunction with the development of a politically sustainable social contract.

28. The Poverty Reduction Strategy Paper process is being revisited in the light of the Millennium Development Goals and other commitments made at United Nations conferences and summits and their follow-up processes, with particular emphasis on promoting comprehensive measures that produce tangible benefits for poor people. In this context, more systematic consideration should be given to waiving user fees to ensure that poor people will have access to basic services such as primary education, preventive health care and clean water, or scholarships should be provided so that poor children can attend school.

Rights-based approaches and rights deficit

29. The special status attached to the language of human rights gives a universal moral authority to social claims that would otherwise rest on a value judgement. However, the cases analysed in chapter VI suggest that the force of law arises not so much from existing provisions that obligate the States, but from the social contract on which that law is based. In the absence of such social consensus, there seems to be little hope for enforcing existing entitlements as evidenced by the reluctance of States to join, or to enforce, a very large number of binding international instruments dealing with economic, social and cultural rights. In fact, the connection between social development in general and the International Covenant on Economic, Social and Cultural Rights remains tenuous at best and non-existent at worst.

30. The legal status of indigenous peoples as well as the scope of jurisdiction accorded to States under treaties between the States and indigenous peoples should be clarified.

31. Innovative legal approaches are needed, at both the national and international levels, to address the issue of indigenous land rights, including how to incorporate indigenous peoples' communal ways of life into land rights solutions; how to protect the culture of indigenous peoples; and how to resolve the inconsistency between mainstream intellectual property rights and the traditional forms of collective ownership.

32. The Agreement on Trade-Related Aspects of Intellectual Property Rights (TRIPS) should be amended to better protect indigenous knowledge and resources.

33. New legal frames of reference for immigration should be developed, at both the national and international levels, that take into account the complex nature and dynamics of current flows of migrants. An international consensus should be sought on the basic rights of migrants. Enforcement of the basic rights of migrants should be moved to the top of the human rights agenda. International guidelines for the treatment of undocumented migrants should be developed.

34. The decision as to the scope and purpose of the proposed convention on the rights of persons with disabilities, particularly in respect of the relation between the convention and other general human rights instruments should be informed by a realistic assessment of the contribution of those instruments to social development and the protection and empowerment of major social groups.

Reduction of vulnerabilities, need for policy coherence and international cooperation

35. The basis for social vulnerability, as it is defined in the present report, is economic insecurity. Thus, economic growth and employment creation should be given due consideration in the policy steps taken to reduce social vulnerability, reflecting the emphasis placed on poverty reduction in the Millennium Declaration. However, experience has shown that the trickle-down effect of economic growth per se cannot be relied upon to remedy social problems.

36. Social vulnerability is a complex phenomenon with its causes rooted in social, economic and cultural institutions and practices. As a result, approaches to policy aimed at reducing social vulnerability must be multi-pronged and internally consistent: an integration of social and economic policy is a necessity to alleviate the impact of vulnerabilities on affected individuals, households, communities and social groups. However, that does not imply that policy measures have to be implemented simultaneously or that prioritization is impossible. Quite to the contrary, focus and priorities are necessary for policy to be effective, especially in today's general environment of limited public sector resources. To maximize the effectiveness of policy responses, policy makers need to take an integrated approach to the problem while keeping the appropriate priorities. The approach requires an understanding of the complex relationships among the various dimensions and causes of social vulnerability as well as the development of new and effective ways to coordinate the delivery of economic and social policies.

37. Although sound economic policy is essential, enhancement of the capacity of excluded groups to make demands on service provision and effect policy change is of paramount importance to the reduction of social vulnerabilities, as is assertive public intervention to promote social cohesion.

38.   Furthermore, institutional capacity-building and the development of some form of social protection are important steps for developing countries to take to deal with the consequences of modernization and globalization. In developed countries, reforms of the pension system and other programmes of social protection also need to take into account the changes that are occurring with regard to population ageing, the family and the increased movement of goods, capital and people between countries. Finally, targeted, informed and participative policies are also necessary in addressing specific dimensions of social vulnerability.

Introduction

39. The inspiration for the *Report on the World Social Situation, 2003* is, foremost, the first Millennium Development Goal: to halve, by the year 2015, the proportion of the world's population whose income is less than one dollar a day.[1] However, the *Report* is not about poverty eradication per se. Rather, it tries to discover who those poor people are; what risks and uncertainties they face; and how policies can reduce, if not eliminate, those risks and uncertainties and thereby poverty.

40. At present, 1.2 billion people are living in absolute poverty. However compelling in absolute numbers and appalling from an income point of view, the aggregation, the lumping together and the ultimate anonymity of those who are conveniently called "the poor" fail to describe the dismal conditions under which poor people live and the vulnerabilities to which they are exposed.

41. The *Report*, therefore, proceeds in a different direction. The course set out is to examine a number of social groups — older persons, youth, the disabled, indigenous peoples, migrants and persons in situations of conflict, with due consideration to gender-specific issues — among whom the incidence of poverty and deprivation is particularly high. Clearly, those social groups do not exhaust the universe of those who are poor, nor are they mutually exclusive (except for older persons and youth), but what they do represent are people with an unusual degree of vulnerability to events outside their control because of their high level of social and economic dependency.[2]

42. All social groups identified in the *Report* are concerned about the risk and reality of social vulnerability they face. The specific expressions of their common concern may take different forms from one group to another, but the consensus is that social vulnerability forms a barrier to the full realization of their potential and robs them of their voice and rights.

43. The social groups concerned — but, of course, not all members of each group — suffer from the same vicious circle: non-participation — powerlessness — social and economic deprivation — vulnerability. Persons with a disability face enormous barriers, both physical and attitudinal, to integration into mainstream society. The risks of illiteracy, unemployment and delinquency faced by youth are also expressions of their social vulnerability — the lack of access to education and employment, and alienation from society. Migrants are "outsiders" in their host countries, often excluded from social benefits and services available to nationals, and face other cultural, linguistic and social barriers to full social integration. Their rights are not a high priority on the political agenda; they even have a tendency to live in segregated immigrant enclaves. Older persons are challenged by decreased mobility, and modern societies often do not offer sufficient social support in place of lost family and community networks that used to give them a sense of belonging. They also face age discrimination in the job market. The plight of indigenous peoples is perhaps the most glaring. They are often stereotyped as backward and ignorant, shunned by the mainstream society. They see economic development projects exploiting the natural resources of their lands, often without their input when decisions are made. The sense of isolation felt by indigenous peoples in their own native environment and their powerlessness against the "outside" world highlights their social vulnerability. Violent conflicts destroy structures of social support and governance, put civilian lives in danger, disrupt children's education and the delivery of other social services, and often lead to internal displacement and refugee flows. Warring parties do not respect the rights and voice of innocent people caught in conflict situations. As a result, they are among the most vulnerable.

44. The *Report* gives the reader insights into the plight of those living on the margins of society. The lack of policies and measures to bring them into the mainstream can only be seen as a major policy failure of the Governments of all countries, whether developed, developing or in transition, as well as of the international community, which in the eighth Millennium Development Goal committed itself to develop a global partnership for development.

---

[1] The goal is set out in the Millennium Declaration (General Assembly resolution 55/2 of 8 September 2000) and is derived from the World Summit for Social Development of 1995 and the twenty-fourth special session of the General Assembly, entitled "World Summit for Social Development and beyond: achieving social development for all in a globalizing world".

[2] Selected indicators of vulnerability by country are presented in the annex tables.

45. The first and eighth Millennium Development Goals are inextricably linked. However, as the *Report* shows, making the linkage explicit and operational is highly complex. The largely macroeconomic policies embedded in the eighth goal are not easily translated into reality for the social groups and individuals who live in poverty and suffer from vulnerability.

46. The World Summit for Social Development put people at the centre of development. That meant **all** people, not some of the people. However, as the present report makes abundantly clear, that aim is still a long way from becoming a reality. The disenfranchised, the powerless and the voiceless are still largely relegated to the periphery, and making them part of the centre is not just a challenge but an obligation — morally, socially and economically.

47. The goal of the *Report* is to make a case: to be an advocate for the forgotten, the invisible and the ignored billions of poor people, so they will be included in and integrated into the development process as a matter of course and right.

Vulnerability: an overview

48. Since the mid-1990s, reference has often been made to the notion of vulnerability in the context of social policy. At the simplest level, vulnerability is an intuitively appealing notion that seems to fit well into the discussion of many social issues. Use of the words "vulnerability" and "vulnerable" has been quite loose in policy contexts and has been accompanied by neither the theoretical rigour nor the degree of elaboration that one finds in analytical works.

49. As a consequence, the term "vulnerability" has a wide variety of meanings. Vulnerability stems from many sources and can be traced to multiple factors rooted in physical, environmental, socio-economic and political causes. In essence, vulnerability can be seen as a state of high exposure to certain risks and uncertainties, in combination with a reduced ability to protect or defend oneself against those risks and uncertainties and cope with their negative consequences.[3] It exists at all levels and dimensions of society and forms an integral part of the human

condition, affecting both individuals and society as whole.

50. While situation-specific vulnerabilities are very important, the main emphasis in the present report is on group-specific vulnerabilities and, consequently, on the challenges of social inclusion. That approach helps to identify the barriers that prevent social integration for those groups.

51. In 2000, there were 1.8 billion children and 1.1 billion youth, together accounting for 47 per cent of the global population. Eighty-eight per cent of the world's children live in developing countries. A staggering 40 per cent of those children, estimated at well over half a billion, are struggling to survive on less than one dollar a day. Older persons — those aged 60 and over — numbered 606 million worldwide, with 60 per cent of them living in developing countries. The most recent estimates put the global number of long-term migrants (those living abroad for over a year) at 175 million; in developed countries, almost 1 out of every 10 persons is a migrant. The total number of persons with disabilities is about 600 million, including 385 million persons of working age. Between 300 to 500 million people are considered to be indigenous, worldwide. The latter two groups are often among the poorest of the poor and the most marginalized sectors of population.

52. Although the numbers obviously cannot simply be added together, what they nevertheless make abundantly clear is that large proportions of the groups represent the majority of those addressed in the first Millennium Development Goal. Moreover, the poor among them are often the most vulnerable. In order to make progress in achieving that Goal, policy interventions would greatly benefit if they took into account who the poor really are.

53. Although the phrase "vulnerable groups" continues to be included routinely in policy documents, civil society organizations have expressed increasing uneasiness with this language. Reference to social groups' overall vulnerability is more and more found to be socially and politically inaccurate and misleading, since a number of groups are engaged in promoting policy agendas that focus on their empowerment and participation in development. The common argument is that no social group is inherently vulnerable. However, all groups face vulnerabilities that are largely the outcome of economic, social and cultural barriers

---

[3] See "Reducing vulnerability", *Report on the World Social Situation, 2001*, chap. XIII (United Nations publication, Sales No. E.01.IV.5).

restricting opportunities for and impeding the social integration and participation of the members of the groups.

54. Common to the analysis of vulnerabilities among the different groups is the existence of some form of discrimination and exclusion that is not primarily market-related or market-generated but socially generated. Members of the groups are unable to make a full contribution to society because of cultural biases, customs, social indifference or antagonism. The emphasis on social relations between various groups and the society at large also point to the clear role of poverty as a source or correlate of vulnerability.

55. Vulnerability and poverty interact with each other, creating a vicious circle in which the two reinforce each other. Poor people are the most vulnerable to economic shocks, material losses and losses of well-being. Such events can easily destroy their ability to move out of poverty, both in the long run and in the short run, by depleting their human and physical assets, a process that may be irreversible. An increase in vulnerability especially affects poor people because they have greater exposure to many downward risks (such as illness, death, loss of employment or famine), and they are less capable of responding to them. Poverty and inequalities also may increase vulnerability indirectly by fuelling social tensions and undermining the social cohesion needed to pre-empt and respond to emerging dangers.

56. The reduction of vulnerabilities among the whole population, but especially among the groups that are the subject of the *Report*, is therefore a crucial element in a country's fight against poverty. Reducing their exposure to vulnerabilities gives people a better chance in the struggle to improve their socio-economic status so they do not have to direct all their efforts to the reduction of those vulnerabilities. In addition, it avoids undoing the efforts that have already been made to improve their poverty status, should their vulnerability increase.

57. Identifying and protecting the most vulnerable during episodes of increased risk, such as macroeconomic crises, natural disasters and famine is therefore essential to poverty reduction in both developed and developing countries. During those times, such policies and measures as the creation of well-targeted emergency programmes that provide income support to the most needy and the maintenance of already existing social programmes are particularly essential.

58. While vulnerability, uncertainty and insecurity are not new in people's lives, what is new is that the causes and manifestations of those elements have multiplied and changed profoundly over the last decade. Examples include civil strife and the proliferation of conflicts; growing inequalities within and among countries, further accentuated by globalization; mixed outcomes of poverty reduction efforts; increased mobility of populations; and changes in family structures.

59. During the last two decades of the twentieth century, for example, there were a total of 164 violent conflicts affecting 89 countries for an average of six to seven years.[4] Conflicts tend to be concentrated in poorer countries: more than half of all low-income countries have experienced significant conflicts since 1990. The greatest impact has been in Africa, where virtually every country or an immediate neighbour has suffered a major conflict over the last decade.[5] Where violent conflict occurs, economic development is set back because industries are destroyed, social services are abandoned, agricultural areas are laid waste and already poor populations are faced with the threat of famine. The past decades have also witnessed a change in the nature of the conflicts, with a greater likelihood of conflict emerging within States rather than between States.

60. Increasingly, fighting parties sustain themselves by taking control of natural resources and civilian assets. That new economy of war has led to a proliferation of armed groups organized with weak command-and-control lines. As a result, untrained combatants have waged most of the recent wars in disregard (and probably ignorance) of the Geneva Conventions that include provisions for the protection of civilians. Civilians have been used as tools of battle in various ways, including the expulsion or massacre of populations and the rape of women, in order to gain

---

[4] Heidelberg Institute of International Conflict Research (HIIK), *Database KOSIMO (1945-1999)*, last updated 8 November 2002 (Heidelberg, Germany, University of Heidelberg). Available from http://www.hiik.de

[5] World Bank, *World Development Report, 2003: Sustainable Development in a Dynamic World: Transforming Institutions, Growth and Quality of Life* (New York, Oxford University Press, and Washington, D.C., the World Bank, 2002).

control over resource-rich territories, to hasten a surrender or simply to gain leverage over the "enemy". Children and refugee populations have served as human shields or have been recruited as combatants. Combatants have also restricted civilian access to food and/or other forms of life-saving assistance.

61. As a result, traditional forms of power at the community level that served as local conflict resolution mechanisms have been challenged. Informal power structures have been losing their relevance in many societies as modernization erodes the very foundations of such power. One of the dire consequences of such social change is the loss of social cohesion based on traditions.

62. Globalization is another important development, which has considerable implications for vulnerability. The process of globalization has been cited as a major source of impoverishment and social exclusion, particularly in developing countries, which lack the capacity for local responses to its adverse economic and social consequences. The detractors of globalization argue that the benefits do not accrue to all countries equally and that there are countries that are marginalized in the globalization process — those countries receive little, if any, foreign direct investment (FDI) and their share of world trade is negligible. Of the countries that do receive FDI, the benefits of globalization tend to be highly localized and do not reach the wider community, especially the poor and disadvantaged. The vulnerability of poor people in economies excluded from or marginalized in the globalization process increases as they are cut off from opportunities. However, even those countries that are benefiting from the process of globalization find that segments of their populations, particularly those who are poor and socially excluded, are increasingly vulnerable to economic and financial volatility.

63. Another consideration is the effect that globalization has on social cohesion. As the existence of social cohesion has proven to be a mitigating factor against the forces that lead to increased vulnerability, the question arises as to whether the forces of globalization are overwhelming or at least undermining social cohesion, leading to social exclusion, various forms of anomie and other negative changes affecting the fabric of society. There is increasing evidence that a combination of ongoing economic liberalization and other trends, such as the ageing of the population, changing family structures and continuous

urbanization, has not only put traditional social protection mechanisms (including formal social security, social welfare services and informal family support systems) under pressure, but has further eroded the ability of individuals, households, groups and communities to cope with hardship, thereby increasing their vulnerability.

64. The ability to cope with the impact of adverse events matters, not only in determining the degree of ex post, outcome-based vulnerability, but also in influencing the state of mind of the vulnerable (or the degree of ex ante vulnerability). In general, greater capacity to cope reduces the negative impact of risks on welfare. Stronger coping capacity would also help alleviate the sense of victimization and the fear of vulnerability.

65. Owing to their lack of resources, people at or near the threshold of poverty are unable to withstand shocks since they are barely surviving, and any adverse event that reduces their income further can push them over the edge. For instance, people whose livelihoods are dependent on the export of primary commodities, such as many poor farmers in developing countries, are highly vulnerable to the downward trend and volatility of the prices of primary commodities in the world market. To contend with the price shocks, poor farmers often have to resort to informal coping mechanisms to address the loss of income, which may include taking children out of school and putting them to work, cutting back on their food intake and selling productive assets. Such short-term coping strategies can end up having long-term negative consequences, particularly when they take the form of reductions in health and education investments for children, factors that can perpetuate the cycles of poverty and exclusion.

66. Compounding the problem is that Governments, in response to crises, often put in place economic reforms that have a disproportionate impact on poor people. Fiscal austerity measures, for example, have led to cutbacks in public assistance and social protection, leaving poor people even more vulnerable because they have neither the private nor the public resources needed to help them cope with the crisis at hand. Furthermore, structural adjustment policies implemented following a crisis often result in massive cutbacks in public sector employment, greatly contributing to the unemployment problem already spurred by the economic downturn. Left without jobs, sufficient savings or an adequate safety net to see them

through the crisis, a greater number of people become vulnerable to falling into poverty.

67. Moreover, many of the social institutions that serve as mitigating factors against the impact of adverse conditions and events have undergone dramatic changes in the recent past. In the process, their mitigating functions in the broader social context have been eroded. One such social institution is the family.

68. The last decade has continued to bring changes in family structures, including an increase in mobility, which has further contributed to vulnerability for some populations. In traditional societies the family unit is often the first line of defence in the event of disasters. It also has the function of caring for the young and the old, protecting them against risks that they cannot manage alone. The rise of the nuclear family, accompanying industrialization and urbanization, has weakened the family's capacity to provide a social protection network the way the extended family used to. Its role in caring for and protecting the old has also been eroded as intergenerational living arrangements have gone out of favour. Another result of industrialization and urbanization is the migration of the young from rural areas. That trend has created a high concentration of poor older persons without the support of adult children in rural areas in both developed and developing countries, making the older persons more vulnerable to fluctuations in income. Furthermore, the size of the nuclear family has been declining, reducing the number of close family relatives. The consequence of that demographic change has been the reduction of the capability of families to meet the financial and care needs of the older generation at a time when the older generation most needs such support from their families.

69. Furthermore, poor health forces poor families to choose between using their limited resources on the care of the sick, making other family members more vulnerable to poverty, or leaving their sick untreated and suffering the consequences. It is quite common for families with limited resources to fall dangerously close to or into poverty once a member becomes ill. The human immunodeficiency virus/acquired immunodeficiency syndrome (HIV/AIDS) epidemic is only one example of health-related vulnerability. HIV/AIDS renders individuals and their families extremely vulnerable. The devastation that the HIV/AIDS epidemic is causing in many poor countries in sub-Saharan Africa demonstrates the impact of ill

health on social vulnerability. Individuals with HIV/AIDS face discrimination, while their families are stigmatized. Medical expenses to treat a family member with the infection and lost earnings have left countless families financially ruined. Young children become AIDS orphans, facing additional emotional, financial and security challenges at a young age.

70. In view of the preceding remarks, assessing susceptibility to vulnerability provides a new way of approaching such issues as poverty eradication and social protection. Vulnerability assessment highlights who is susceptible, how susceptible and why. It also reflects a life course approach, which recognizes that a person's vulnerability can shift, change and build up throughout the course of his or her life.

71. Social protection provides a useful example of how vulnerability assessment can be applied, particularly from the perspective of one's changing needs over the course of a lifetime. Access to social protection is necessary to attenuate, reduce, mitigate, cope and insure against socially unacceptable levels of risk and vulnerability, and it is a need that continues throughout the life course. Children need access to health care and education; young people and adults need income support during periods of joblessness; those suffering from poverty need assistance in maintaining minimum standards of living, including access to adequate housing and nutrition and safe drinking water; and older people need some kind of income security during the final period of their lives. The life course perspective on the provision of social protection considers that people, whether individually or as members of a group, qualify for certain rights at any point in their lives, including the entitlements of access to health care, lifelong work or income support, non-discrimination and equality of opportunity, and continuous education and learning.

72. The degree to which an individual or group is dependent upon social protection to achieve and sustain those rights at any stage in their life can be viewed as a function of the individual's or group's vulnerability. Conversely, the degree of access to social protection plays an important role in minimizing the level and extent of an individual's or group's vulnerability during their life course.

73. The distribution of income and wealth and access to formal and informal social protection arrangements are the fundamental material and social conditions that

define vulnerability for some households and security for others. Livelihood vulnerability, therefore, can vary according to social class, gender, race and ethnicity and age; degree of powerlessness; and nature of actions by the State to promote or restrict livelihood opportunities. Clearly, sufficient economic resources under command can always compensate for the impact of adverse shocks so that welfare remains above the minimal threshold. Thus, similar natural disasters hitting countries with similar geographical conditions often result in very different losses in welfare, for countries with different income levels have different abilities to manage the impact. Similarly, well-off senior citizens in affluent societies do not face the same challenges or daily struggle as poor older people or older people in general in developing countries, although their vulnerabilities have some common dimensions.

74. Socially produced vulnerability has its roots in powerlessness. Marginalization and social exclusion underlie social, political and economic powerlessness and perpetuate the perception of vulnerability. The risk of social exclusion contributes most directly to social vulnerability. Without effective participation in socio-economic decision-making processes, social groups and individuals lack the means to make their concerns and interests heard. Not only does this result in the implementation of policies and programmes that fail to benefit, or actually conflict with, the social and economic interests of the politically powerless, it also undermines or destroys the very livelihood of individuals, families, communities and groups, weakening their cultural identities and social structure.

75. While there is little agreement on the exact meaning of the term "social exclusion", there is general agreement on its core features, its principal indicators and its relationship to poverty and inequality. For instance, there is very little opposition to the view that poverty, when defined by a wider set of circumstances than income poverty, is a central component of social exclusion. Social exclusion is perceived as being more closely related to the concept of relative, rather than absolute, poverty and is therefore linked with inequality. Social exclusion extends beyond this broad, multidimensional view of poverty to include social deprivation and a lack of voice and power in society. Various forms of exclusion occur in combination, including exclusion from participation in political processes and decision-making; exclusion from access to employment and material resources; and exclusion from integration into common cultural processes.

76. To achieve a reduction in social vulnerability, it is important to gain an understanding of the factors and forces that lie at its source. A fundamental question concerns what makes an individual or group vulnerable — or at greater risk of becoming vulnerable — to a variety of social ills. Both internal and external dynamics are at play in determining one's level of vulnerability, encompassing a variety of economic, social and environmental concerns. Proper identification of trends and driving forces, coupled with an assessment of the underlying causes leading to structural vulnerabilities, can provide a proper basis for well-considered and balanced policy action. Anchoring the policy response to empowerment and social integration increases the chances of success in the long run. It is to the issues of sources of, and policy responses to, social vulnerability that the remainder of the *Report* is devoted.

Part one
Sources and manifestations of vulnerability

Introduction

77.   The sources of vulnerability are as diverse as its many meanings. One approach is to investigate those sources by social group. However, many of the sources will be common to the groups in question, risking repetition. It is possible to take a different approach: categorize the social groups by their sources of vulnerability. The latter approach has the added advantage that policy prescriptions can yield multiple results: they are not necessarily specific to any one group but can be beneficial for more than one group at the same time.

78.   In part I of the *Report on the World Social Situation, 2003*, the sources of vulnerability are used, to the greatest extent possible, to categorize the social groups concerned. Inevitably, there are sources of vulnerability that are unique and group-specific. When such situations arise, they have been identified by means of subsections in the chapters that follow.

79.   Certainly, any clustering or classification of sources of vulnerability can be neither exhaustive nor comprehensive. Furthermore, the sources identified here — income insecurity, social ills, and sociocultural biases and discrimination — do not operate truly independently from each other. Their separation, therefore, introduces a certain degree of artificiality but, from a policy perspective, helps to facilitate the design of policy interventions.

I. Income insecurity

Labour market exclusion and globalization

80. Lack of access to gainful employment is the most common concern of all social groups and is one of the most important sources of vulnerability. For young people, limited employment opportunities are a key concern, as their unemployment rate is typically two to three times that of adults. For older persons, the lack of meaningful jobs not only wastes a valuable productive resource at the societal level, it also poses risks of poverty and dependency in old age. From the perspective of persons with disabilities, access to employment is at the core of their rights and vital for their integration into mainstream society. Among the concerns and vulnerabilities of international migrants, employment-related issues are part and parcel of the protection of migrants' rights and their overall well-being. A large number of indigenous people live in areas where there are typically few or no jobs; therefore, expanding opportunities for employment is critical to indigenous livelihoods. In conflict prevention as well as in post-conflict reconstruction, employment creation plays an important role in mitigating social tension, rehabilitating former combatants and helping to rebuild war-torn areas.

81. Unemployment, underemployment and job insecurity are the causes as well as the outcomes of the social vulnerability suffered by various groups. Lack of employment and job security can result in income insecurity and poverty, which in turn contribute to social vulnerability through social discrimination, greater exposure to risks and weak coping capacity. Poor people are often employed in informal sectors where working conditions are not regulated and wages are quite low. Poor people are also more likely to live and work in unsafe, unsanitary conditions. Access to education and health services for them is limited, and the quality of the services they do receive is often substandard, especially in developing countries. Those conditions result in low educational attainment and poor health and increase their exposure to injuries, malnutrition and diseases, further reinforcing their social isolation and increasing their level of social vulnerability.

Box 1

Assessing vulnerabilities: income poverty

Poverty as measured by income is most prevalent in sub-Saharan Africa, where, on average, 51 per cent of the population (324 million people) live on less than one dollar per day. In a few countries in the region, the figure is over 70 per cent.

In South Asia the figures are also alarming: on average, 32 per cent live on less than one dollar per day. South Asia accounts for the largest proportion of the world's population living on less than one dollar per day — approximately 40 per cent, or about 437 million people.

Source: World Bank, *World Development Indicators, 2003* (Washington, D.C., 2003).

---

82. An important factor hampering the participation of poor people in formal labour markets is, ironically, poverty itself. Poor people are more likely to suffer from ill health and inadequate nutrition than those who are not poor, factors that limit their ability to gain entry into and to remain in the relatively small formal labour markets of developing countries. Education is another key consideration, as poor households typically have unequal educational opportunities or, in some cases, none at all. Family income needs often curtail children's school attendance, as young people are pushed into the workforce prematurely, preventing them from attaining the knowledge and skills they need

to compete for better, more productive jobs in the formal labour market.

83. Macroeconomic policies, including fiscal policy, international trade and financial liberalization, and employment policy, all influence social vulnerability. Fiscal policy directly affects income distribution and the financial resources allocated to social sectors, and it therefore has an impact on both risk and its mitigation. International trade and financial liberalization, if active labour market policies are absent, can lead to real or perceived employment insecurity. Related to the recent trends in financial liberalization, change has come about through the growing imbalance in bargaining power between employers and unions, which has produced downward pressures on wages and job security, at least in economic sectors where international competition has intensified.

84. Persistent unemployment in many developed countries has generated greater labour market insecurity, particularly in Europe. At the same time, the gap between the wages of skilled and unskilled workers has widened. There is strong support for the view that the market forces responsible for the rapid spread of globalization have been a major contributory factor to the increased vulnerability of workers. In particular, the rise in vulnerability among workers is often attributed to the decline in manufacturing employment following the surge of manufacturing exports from developing to developed countries.

85. In that context, there is evidence that the "standard" employment relationship is declining in favour of more precarious forms of employment that typically offer lower wages, poorer working conditions and less social protection.

86. Furthermore, significant changes in family dynamics and work patterns have taken place that challenge existing formal and informal support systems. The labour force participation rates of women are quickly approaching those of men, and workers on the whole exhibit differing work patterns, as many people cycle in and out of the formal labour force over the course of their working lives. People may move from informal work, such as subsistence farming, to more formalized employment in urban areas, or they may take time out to raise children or care for older family members. Moreover, people are more mobile today than ever before, with increasing numbers of individuals and families migrating both within and between countries. However, State-supported social protection systems, to the limited extent that they exist in the world, have not been modified to accommodate the changes. Formal social protection systems are largely designed to benefit those with uninterrupted years of service in the formal economy, preferably in the same country and with the same employer.

87. In developed countries, those changes have resulted in a significant increase in employment-related vulnerability in such precarious forms of employment as home-based work, part-time work or temporary work, on-call work or self-employment.[6] Precarious employment is characterized by limited social benefits, limited statutory entitlements, low wages and poor working conditions. It offers no certainty of continuing employment, a high risk of job loss, a low level of regulatory protection and no recognition of trade union rights.[7] In addition, there is a link between changing employment relationships and sex/gender inequalities in the labour market.

88. Nevertheless, the increased vulnerabilities experienced by workers in developed countries cannot be explained by rapid trade liberalization and surges in imports alone; those phenomena are only a part of the globalizing process. The impact of market forces in today's globalizing world arises from a mix of factors, including overall demand conditions, the workings of global financial markets and the role of technological change, in particular the information and communication revolution. Specifically, developments in financial markets have made it easier to establish a global production base, thereby facilitating the relocation of production from high-cost to lower-cost regions. Technological changes ushered in by the information and communication revolution have not only led to labour shedding in industries but have also made it possible to shift certain production and services to lower-cost developing countries. All those

---

[6] International Labour Organization, *World Employment Report 1998-1999* (Geneva, International Labour Office, 1998).

[7] G. Rogers, "Precarious employment in Western Europe: the state of the debate", in *Precarious Jobs in Labour Market Regulation: The Growth of Atypical Employment in Western Europe*, G. Rogers and J. Rogers, editors (Belgium, International Institute for Labour Studies, 1989).

factors further increase the vulnerability of labour in developed countries.

89. The employment picture is even more discouraging for developing countries.[8] A recurring observation is that, although most developing countries have made great efforts to integrate more fully into the world economy, many have not been able to reap the potential benefits from greater trade and investment flows. One explanation for the uneven distribution of the benefits of globalization between developed and developing countries lies in the weaknesses and deficiencies of the current international trading and financial systems, which tend to operate against the interests of developing countries. Beyond that, the steep rise in unemployment and poverty that emerged in the wake of the Asian financial crisis revealed the heightened vulnerability of developing countries to the volatility and change that can occur in global financial markets. The dramatic worsening of labour market conditions during the Asian financial crisis, in even the most robust developing countries, raised serious concerns about the effect of rapid financial market liberalization upon vulnerability among workers and poor people. The impact of financial crises on wages, employment and poverty in Asia was similar to that experienced during earlier episodes in Latin America. The effect of such crises has been a reduction in real wages, higher unemployment and poverty and, therefore, greater income insecurity.

Box 2

Assessing vulnerabilities: unemployment

The lack of access to gainful employment is an important source of vulnerability. Although unemployment figures alone may not reveal pervasive underemployment or the existence of working poor people, they remain useful indicators. Unemployment in Latin America and the Caribbean and in Europe averages 10 per cent.

The unemployment rate in the OECD countries is 6 per cent, on average.

In most countries, men account for a larger proportion of the labour force than women; however, in many countries the unemployment rate among women is much higher than that of men.

Source: International Labour Organization, *Key Indicators of the Labour Market*, 2001-2002, database (Geneva).

---

90. Labour conditions during the Asian financial crisis eroded sharply, particularly among the unskilled, displaying a significant asymmetry in the impact of growth and crises on poverty in developing countries. The fact that the economic recovery that followed the crisis did not fully reverse the deterioration in labour conditions suggests that the impact of economic growth on poverty reduction is weaker than the impact on poverty of a comparable decline in economic growth.

91. Relying upon the unemployment rate alone as an indicator of employment conditions in developing countries, as is often the case, masks the full extent of vulnerability of the poor in developing countries. The unemployment rate is inadequate, as it fails to reveal either pervasive underemployment or the existence of working poor people. The reality is that much of the world's labour force still relies on agriculture; roughly three quarters of the working poor in developing countries still live in rural areas where the work is often informal, unprotected and unregulated. An

---

[8] The following analysis is based on "Globalization and the labour market", a paper prepared by the secretariat of the United Nations Conference on Trade and Development for the meeting of the ILO Working Party on the Social Dimension of Globalization, Geneva, 12 November 2001 (UNCTAD/GDS/MDPB/Misc.14).

important concern is that in Africa and Asia, women are disproportionately represented in the informal economy and are particularly vulnerable.

92. Conventional economic theory predicts that trade liberalization and greater openness in the world economy should lead to wage convergence between developed and developing countries. Nevertheless, recent evidence from Latin America and sub-Saharan Africa suggests that an increase in unemployment and wage inequality has often accompanied liberalization episodes in many of the developing countries. Indeed, with the exception of the fastest growing developing countries in East Asia, growing wage inequality has been a key outcome of rapid trade liberalization in most developing countries.

93. The picture that presents itself is one of a crisis in employment. While the industrialized countries continue to strongly advocate globalization, liberalization and outward-oriented development, the enduring popular perception in those countries is that labour-market problems are caused by excessive imports of manufactured products from developing countries. The response to the perceived "threat" includes such measures as raising barriers to imports from developing countries, imposing higher labour standards on producers in developing countries and lowering labour standards in their own labour markets. Not only are such responses by developed countries unlikely to resolve all their labour-market problems, the measures will in all probability slow economic growth and industrialization in developing countries.

Youth unemployment

94. Youth unemployment and underemployment should be viewed as a subset of the overall employment problem: the continuous slow growth of productive employment. However, young people are more vulnerable to unemployment and job instability than adults owing to their lack of work experience and professional skills. Young workers tend to serve as buffers in times of economic uncertainty and shock, as they are typically among the first to be fired and the last to be hired during economic downturns.

95. Many young people do not have access to adequate employment, which leads to other risks. Currently, 66 million young people are unemployed worldwide, which constitutes some 40 per cent of the world's unemployed. Although precise figures are not available, it is commonly believed that a significantly larger number of youth are underemployed. Young women are more at risk of becoming unemployed and have unemployment rates that are 20 to 50 per cent higher than that of young men. Whether they live in developed or developing countries, young people suffer disproportionally high levels of unemployment — between two and three times that of older generations — and are increasingly likely to be engaged in precarious, informal or hazardous forms of work. Perpetuating this situation is clearly unacceptable.

96. The case for increasing youth employability through investment in education and vocational training for young people can be made on the basis of two arguments. First, evidence from a wide range of countries shows that education clearly enhances young people's prospects in the labour market. Second, in the long term, the capacity of countries to develop economically and socially and take advantage of globalization will depend on the quality and skills of their labour force. However, operationalization of the relationship between education and employability has proven difficult.

97. In many countries, particularly developing countries, large numbers of highly educated young men and women remain unemployed owing to an inability to match university degrees with demand for corresponding occupations. The phenomenon can be explained primarily by a lack of development in modern sectors of the economy. As the majority of new job growth is in the informal sectors of the economy, few opportunities remain for young people graduating from school to find jobs that correspond to their level of educational attainment. Many of those highly educated workers, therefore, end up migrating to industrialized countries in search of better job prospects. The situation is compounded by an overabundance of students graduating with degrees in the social sciences and humanities, areas in which the number of jobs is insufficient. In contrast, few graduate in such disciplines as engineering and the physical sciences, which require more sophisticated equipment and technology, often too costly for many universities in developing countries to provide.

98. The experience in developed countries in their attempt to increase the employability of youth through education and training provides further evidence of the

difficulty of the challenge. Since the 1990s, a wide variety of youth employment measures have been implemented by the Organisation for Economic Cooperation and Development (OECD) countries as part of what has become known as active labour market policies. Typical measures include formal classroom training, on-the-job training and job-search assistance, which may include individual counselling, job clubs, Internet job postings, employment incentives (bonuses), employment subsidies and direct youth job creation in both the public and private sectors. A major and disheartening conclusion of recent assessments of what works among active policies and for whom is that youth measures have proven to be the least effective of any form of labour market policy.[9] A positive impact on any significant scale has not been observed in terms of either employment prospects or wages for out-of-school young people. Only a few examples of successful measures have been found locally in the handful of countries that have been the most successful in terms of overall employment creation.

99.   Young people also remain largely barred from access to entrepreneurship, a critical issue in developing countries where self-employment is often the only choice for survival. Owing to their lack of collateral and business experience, lenders consider youth very high-risk clients, making it difficult for them to borrow money. In a context where many employers value skills and experience, a proven work ethic and the ability to perform on the job, young people, particularly those with limited education or training, are at disadvantage in the search for employment. However, that disadvantage is too often reinforced by gender biases and by negative attitudes towards the employment of young people who come from socially excluded communities or who represent ethnic minorities.

Employment and working conditions of migrants

100.   Although policy attention has been mostly devoted to "organizing" the immigration of highly skilled workers who meet specific labour needs, the majority of migrants have low qualifications and occupy jobs at the bottom end of the wage scale. Deception, discrimination, exploitation and sometimes abuse are employment-related situations commonly and increasingly faced by poorly skilled migrant workers.[10] The vulnerability of migrants may be explained in part by the current xenophobic climate in many societies; however, that vulnerability arises primarily from the migrants position in the labour market and the lack of application and enforcement of labour standards in host countries.

101.   The gap in labour standards is largely the result of the simultaneous occurrence of two trends. First, in the 1990s the number of host countries increased significantly, particularly among the developing countries. Many of those countries had neither provisions for minimum working conditions nor migration laws.[11] Second, especially in developed countries with low enforcement of standards for occupational safety and working conditions, such labour-intensive sectors as agriculture, construction, domestic employment, low-skilled manufacturing industries, the informal sector and the "sex industry" rely increasingly on imported, and often undocumented, labour.

102.   Labour market deregulation has allowed a large number of undocumented migrants to find jobs despite relatively high levels of unemployment in developed countries. At the same time, employment-related discrimination has made it more difficult for legitimate migrants to find or change jobs. Although evidence is currently sparse, discrimination against migrants as well as ethnic minorities is a worldwide phenomenon. Studies carried out by the International Labour

[9] J. P. Martin and D. Grubb, "What works and for whom: a review of OECD countries' experiences with active labour market policies", *Swedish Economic Policy Review, 2001*, vol. 8, No. 1.

[10] See P. Taran and E. Geronimi, *Globalization, Labour and Migration: Protection is Paramount* (Geneva, International Labour Office, 2003).

[11] Based on the entries in the NATLEX database maintained by the International Labour Organization, over 100 countries enacted legislation or signed agreements that related to migration during the 1990s. In comparison, in 1970 there were only approximately 40 countries employing foreign labour.

Organization (ILO) in four European countries found that more than one in three job applications by immigrants and members of minorities were rejected or not given consideration.[12]

103. Migrants working under substandard conditions offer a low-cost and flexible manpower alternative for small and medium-sized companies that cannot relocate their operations abroad. The presence of large numbers of undocumented migrants, an unintended consequence of restrictive immigration policies, has fuelled the trend. In a sense, migrants' vulnerability makes it possible to exploit them further.

104. Migrants' economic rights are almost completely contingent on immigration laws and are usually limited. For migrants in many countries, both their access to labour markets and the scope of their engagement in professions and trade are restricted. Those restrictions may apply during a limited period of time. In many countries, migrants cannot change employers or jobs during their first year of residence, and the restriction usually applies permanently to migrants recruited under guest worker contracts.

105. While immigration laws dictate migrants' economic rights, they rarely contain provisions for the enforcement of those rights. This creates a particular problem for migrants who are expelled or for those who try to recover any employment-related outstanding payment after they have left the host country upon termination of employment.

106. In a few countries, migrants have begun organizing themselves in order to assert their rights, sometimes with the help of non-governmental organizations. In addition, in a number of developed countries, the threat posed by deregulation to the enforcement of labour standards and concerns with plummeting membership have led labour unions to adopt more open views towards immigration and the plight of migrants.

107. Furthermore, Governments of the sending countries, particularly in Asia, have been increasingly concerned about the mistreatment and abuse of their nationals employed overseas and have become more actively involved in migration issues. Some countries

---

[12] R. Zegers de Beijl, editor, *Documenting Discrimination against Migrant Workers in the Labour Market: A Comparative Study of Four European Countries* (Geneva, International Labour Office, 2000).

have adopted measures for the protection of their nationals, including insurance schemes, and many Asian embassies now have labour attachés on their staff. This has also led public authorities to review existing institutional arrangements for emigration. Although bilateral agreements exist between some sending and receiving countries in parts of Western Asia, they have had little impact. On the receiving side, some countries of Western Asia acknowledge that their migration legislation and practices are outdated and inadequate and require updating and/or reformulation. Regional cooperation between receiving and sending countries has been contemplated but implementation has lagged behind.

108. Such factors as differences in language, skills, education and professional experience, a lack of social networks, and residence in neighbourhoods that are densely populated by migrants and minorities contribute to the difficulties that migrants, particularly young migrants, encounter in finding jobs. Furthermore, there is some evidence that immigrants tend to be among the first to be laid off during times of economic difficulties, while they are the last to be rehired later. Unemployment rates among immigrant workers are high in many Western European countries. During the recent Asian economic crisis, many migrants, particularly legal migrants, lost their jobs. In contrast, the foreign manpower employed in export sectors that benefited from the devaluations, such as forestry and plantations, increased. Nonetheless, large numbers of regular migrants who lost their jobs moved to lower paid jobs in the informal sector. In the course of the crisis, the informalization of certain economic sectors seems to have attracted new waves of migrants, bringing additional downward pressure on wages.

Social protection, employment and income insecurity among older persons

109. The ageing of the population, along with changes in the workforce dynamics of older persons, have helped shape the debate on pensions. For a handful of highly industrialized countries — with the exception of older widows, who fare less well — older persons have managed thus far to reach old age without experiencing a dramatic fall in their living standards, regardless of the level of their country's public pension

expenditure.[13] However, it is estimated that over the next quarter century, some 70 million people will retire in OECD countries and be replaced by only 5 million new workers. In contrast, during the previous quarter century, 45 million new pensioners were replaced in the workforce by 120 million workers.[14]

110. Public scrutiny surrounding the high administrative costs of many existing pension schemes, which can quickly eat into returns, has galvanized experts to urge caution — as well as good governance and transparency — when developing a plan's architecture. According to some, the OECD countries have not moved aggressively to address system cost and stability issues, and it is further felt that the increasing debt implicit in some systems, particularly the application of current pay-as-you-go rules, will lead to higher contributions for workers and/or higher income taxes for both workers and pensioners.[15]

111. For many countries, pension reform has to contend with economic crises and high levels of public debt that not only threaten economic stability but also squeeze out necessary investments in education, health and infrastructure, leaving entire populations at risk. The economic crisis that hit Argentina in 2001 has caused wide and abrupt impoverishment among broad sectors; older persons have suffered a reduction of about 13 per cent in their retirement benefits, devaluation of their lifelong savings and the consequences of the collapse of the *Instituto Nacional de Servicios Sociales para Jubilados y Pensionados* (INSSJP), the largest health and social security institute of its kind in Latin America.[16]

112. According to the International Labour Organization, some 90 per cent of the world's working population is not covered by pension schemes capable of providing adequate retirement income. In the countries of the former Soviet Union, pension schemes have become practically worthless with the collapse of national economies; in Africa, pension schemes are weak in general and poorly managed; in Asia, schemes have been weakened by the continent's financial turmoil of the late 1990s; in the labour-importing countries of the Middle East, foreign workers are not permitted to join the retirement schemes; and in Latin America and the Caribbean, schemes are performing poorly, with a number of countries converting to different systems.[17] For those not covered, or covered by poorly performing pension schemes, old age income is not secured at all.

113. Ongoing questions of how to find a balance between public and private sector responsibility for the provision of old age protection and workers' rights and needs for security also arise in debates over the labour market's ability to absorb and retain workers. While the participation of older persons in the labour market is a pivotal factor in reducing their vulnerability, the overall rate of labour-force participation of older persons has been on a steady decline for decades, even as their numbers and proportions are increasing.

114. Africa and Asia have the highest proportion of older persons who are economically active — over 40 per cent — which translates into very large numbers, yielding a significant economic impact. In most developing countries, most older persons have worked their entire lives in informal settings with few benefits, if any, and meagre incomes. There is no pension account from which to draw a retirement income and very little chance to build one. Poverty is a motivating factor that compels older persons to continue working as long as their health will allow, as farmers, labourers or vendors.

115. At the other end of the spectrum is Europe, where the proportion of economically active older persons averages as low as 5 per cent and where most retire from wage employment at ages that are strictly mandated; persons are penalized with a loss of social

[13] Bernard Casey and Atsuhiro Yamada, Getting Older, Getting Poorer? A Study of the Earnings, Pensions, Assets and Living Arrangements of Older People in Nine Countries, Labour Market and Social Policy Occasional Papers No. 60 (Paris, Organisation for Economic Cooperation and Development, 2002).

[14] Organisation for Economic Cooperation and Development, *Ageing, Housing and Urban Development* (Paris, 2003).

[15] Louise Fox and Edward Palmer, "New approaches to multipillar pension systems: what in the world is going on?", in *New Ideas about Old Age Security: Toward Sustainable Pension Systems in the 21st Century*, Joseph Stiglitz, editor (Washington, D.C., the World Bank, 2001).

[16] Nélida Redondo, "Social health insurance for older people: a comparison of Argentina and the United States" (in Spanish), paper presented at the United

Nations Research Institute for Social Development International Conference, 8-9 April 2002, Madrid.

[17] Colin Gillion and others, editors, *Social Security Pensions: Development and Reform* (Geneva, International Labour Organization, 2000).

Box 3
Assessing vulnerabilities: pension contributions

Over 90 per cent of the world's working population lack pension schemes to provide them with adequate retirement income, according to the International Labour Organization.

In many countries in sub-Saharan Africa, less than 5 per cent of the working-age population contributes to pension schemes.

In contrast, in most countries in Europe and Central Asia, over 60 per cent of the working-age population contributes to pension schemes.

In most OECD countries, over 80 per cent of the working-age population contributes to pension schemes.

Source: ILO and World Bank.

---

security income if they continue to work beyond a certain age. Such policies were designed when retirees were few in number relative to the working population and benefits could be easily provided. With a retiree population living longer and growing by the day, policies are nevertheless encouraging people to shorten their working lives just at a time when they are fit and able to work longer, and are excluding from the labour market those who would prefer to continue working. However, mandatory retirement is only part of the political setting. Unemployment and a lack of opportunities, a demand for mastery of new skills in the expansion of the digital economy and the high value placed on leisure time are also driving the impact of labour market policies with respect to older workers.

116. Over the past two decades, along with women's employment, older women's share of the labour force has been rising, although it is now projected to remain stable at around 10 per cent over the next 10 years. While the total participation rate remains higher for older men, their share is projected to decrease to 18 per cent from 28 per cent today. That rate now ranges from under 2 per cent in some European countries to over 80 per cent in Africa. For older women, the rates range from less than 0.5 per cent in some European countries to more than 60 per cent in African countries.[18] In many countries, however, older women are disproportionately concentrated in low-skill, repetitive jobs, which contributes to their disproportionate representation among poor and vulnerable people.

117. While experts in the field of ageing have debated for decades the effects on society of an ageing population, the global media have recently taken notice, focusing on pension difficulties, population replacement levels and a looming social security and health-care crisis. Underpinning the debate is the global decline in fertility rates, the effect of which is a progressive reduction in the working-age population accompanied by a growing older population. Over the next fifty years, the old-age dependency ratio will almost double in North America, Africa and Oceania; it will more than double in Europe; and more than triple in Asia and in Latin America and the Caribbean. The consequences of those trends are becoming increasingly visible as a result of highly politicized debates that range from immigration and tax policies to the solvency of future pension, social security and health care systems — all with potentially negative implications for the well-being of the older population.

---

[18] "Socio-economic characteristics of the older population", in *World Population Ageing 1950-2050* (United Nations publication, Sales No. E.02.XIII.3).

Employment of persons with disabilities

118. While an estimated 386 million working age people in the world are disabled,[19] they are frequently cut off from employment opportunities and suffer unemployment rates far higher than that of the non-disabled workforce. In many developing countries, it is estimated that 80 per cent or more of the disabled are unemployed, which further contributes to their high incidence of poverty and social exclusion.

119. Approximately one third of disabled persons are not employed owing to severe disabilities in the OECD countries as a whole. Contrary to common belief, the majority of persons with disabilities have the potential to make valuable contributions in the workforce, as employees or as entrepreneurs. In the OECD countries, the average income from work of gainfully employed persons with disabilities differs little from that of people without disabilities. Nonetheless, many disabled persons who are willing and able to work are unemployed.

120. There are basically three reasons for high unemployment among disabled persons. First, the general public perception is that persons with disabilities are unable to work productively, and therefore employers are usually unwilling to give them the opportunity. Second, many workplaces remain inaccessible owing to the lack of appropriate transportation, physical access to buildings or adaptive technology. Third, many adults with disabilities have had limited or no access to general education or training in employable skills.

121. Evidence has shown, however, that not enough attention is currently being paid to improving the employability of disabled persons. A study conducted by the Organisation for Economic Cooperation and Development revealed that people are far more likely to be awarded a disability benefit than receive vocational rehabilitation and training.[20] Vocational

rehabilitation is often not available, either at all or in a timely manner, leaving the disabled in a highly vulnerable position, without employment options and with little control over their livelihood and economic well-being. The OECD study also points to the fact that employment programmes for persons with disabilities have so far played only a minor role in disabled people's employment, although in some countries such programmes seem to have contributed to the employment of the severely disabled.

122. In developed countries, depending on the choice, needs and individual circumstances of persons with disabilities, employment can be provided through one of the following means: open employment, including self-employment; sheltered employment; supported employment; and social enterprises.[21] However, sheltered employment continues to account for the bulk of employment for persons with disabilities despite increasing concerns that sheltered or, for that matter, supported work environments tend to reinforce social exclusion and discrimination.

123. The lack of accessibility to and accommodation within the workplace are major impediments to the employability of persons with disabilities in the open labour market. In the absence of accommodation, such as redesigning workplaces so that they become wheelchair accessible, introducing flexible working hours so that people have time to attend to their medical needs during the workday or preparing workplace instructions so that they are comprehensible to people with visual impairments or intellectual disabilities, the possibility of increasing the employability of persons with disabilities seems remote.

124. The situation is far worse in developing countries, where both disability benefits and vocational rehabilitation services may be virtually non-existent. In such cases, the disabled are often left dependent, destitute and despairing. Given the relatively small size of the formal labour market in most developing countries, particularly in rural areas where many of the disabled live, opportunities for integration of persons

---

[19] International Labour Organization, *Disability and the World of Work*, last updated 5 June 2001, available from http://www.ilo.org/public/english/employment/skills/disability. Based on the estimate by the World Health Organization that 10 per cent of the world's population has a disability, of whom 386 million are between the ages of 15 and 64 years of age.

[20] Christopher Prinz, "Towards a coherent policy mix", paper presented at the OECD Seminar on Active Labour

Market Policies for People with Disabilities, Brussels, 9 July 2002.

[21] Arthur O'Reilly, *The Right to Decent Work of Persons with Disabilities*, IFP/Skills Working Paper No. 14 (Geneva, International Labour Office, 2003).

with disabilities through employment largely rest on informal work, particularly self-employment.

125. Overall, trends in the employment of persons with disabilities are discouraging, whether in the developed or developing countries. Important issues, such as the need to enhance job retention for those who acquire a disability while employed or to facilitate a return to work for those who have left their jobs owing to a disability, have not received sufficient attention by far. Against such a background, changing the perception of disability by the society at large in the near future, so that persons with disability will be recognized as self-supporting and independent members of society, will remain a major challenge.

The challenged livelihoods of indigenous peoples

126. For indigenous peoples, the expropriation of their communal ancestral lands, waters, territories and resources through colonialism and conquest has left a painful legacy of dislocation and displacement and remains the main cause of the destruction of the environment and their way of life.

127. The legal doctrines of dispossession, as part of international law, such as "terra nullius", which views indigenous lands as legally unoccupied until the arrival of a colonial presence, and the doctrine of "discovery", which grants the "discovering" colonial powers free title to indigenous lands subject only to indigenous use and occupancy, have been instrumental in making the expropriation possible. National economic and development priorities of the dominant society are also used to justify the subordination of indigenous peoples' interests in their ancestral lands. In addition, legal systems that protect individual rights often do not protect collective rights, a distinct feature of the way of life of indigenous peoples.

128. The loss of ancestral lands occurs through multiple channels, all of which can be traced to economic development that has encouraged the construction of major infrastructure projects, the opening of forests to loggers, and the encouragement of mining and oil exploration operations in isolated districts, often at considerable cost to indigenous peoples.[22] Their way of life is being eliminated as companies and Governments utilize traditional lands for the extraction of resources, grazing and the generation of hydroelectric power. Economic activities are invariably imposed from the outside; indigenous peoples are not consulted or involved in their implementation, nor do they benefit from them.

129. Dam construction for downstream irrigation and hydroelectric power generation is a typical economic development initiative that leads to the flooding of ancestral lands. To accommodate the construction of dams, indigenous peoples have been resettled or relocated, both voluntarily and involuntarily. However, when satisfactory resettlement schemes are not implemented, indigenous peoples are left without alternative livelihoods.

130. Oil exploration, oil pipelines and mineral extraction and their transportation often also lead to the displacement of indigenous peoples from their ancestral lands. In certain cases, indigenous peoples receive compensation for the use of their land. However, mining and fossil fuel extraction have side effects, including respiratory health problems and environmental degradation.

131. The creation of national parks and reserves is another source of conflict between indigenous peoples and States. Even the conservation programmes pushed by many Governments displace forest dwellers who are still perceived in certain cases as causing the destruction of forests and threatening biodiversity. Furthermore, those conservation programmes, by disregarding indigenous knowledge, can lead to inadvertent forest destruction. In addition Governments grant logging concessions without regard for indigenous peoples, and in several instances, sites have been deforested despite their protected status because Governments use logging concessions for political patronage.[23]

---

[22] "Report of the Expert Seminar on Practical Experiences regarding Indigenous Land Rights and Claims", Whitehorse, Canada, 24-28 March 1996 (E/CN.4/Sub.2/AC.4/1996/6/Add.1).

[23] Victoria Tauli-Corpuz, *The Resistance of the Indigenous Peoples of Asia against Racism and Racial Discrimination* (Baguio City, Philippines, Indigenous Peoples' International Centre for Policy Research and Education, n.d.), available from http://www.tebtebba.org/tebtebba_files/ipr/racism.htm (accessed 4 November 2002).

132. Population growth in the dominant society has also led to encroachment on indigenous peoples' lands. For example, to ease population pressures, in a number of countries transmigration policies that aimed at settling lowland people in indigenous peoples' lands have made the indigenous peoples the minority in their own lands. Not only have those policies resulted in the displacement of indigenous peoples, but they have also often resulted in conflicts between them and the new settlers. In addition, the demand for new lands to accommodate population growth and new sources of raw materials has led to road construction and other infrastructure projects that displace indigenous peoples from their lands. As new areas become more accessible to mainstream society, indigenous peoples are also more easily displaced.

133. In addition, with commercialization and specialization in crop production, subsistence livelihoods are replaced by more volatile sources of income tied to cash crop production on large farms. When cash crops fail, indigenous peoples risk unemployment because they have limited skills and have abandoned subsistence, or more diverse and sustainable, farming methods. Some indigenous farmers have adopted more modern agricultural practices, such as the use of fertilizers, pesticides and modern seeds, to raise productivity. However, with limited financing, lower productivity often occurs since modern seeds are dependent on the right input levels of pesticides and fertilizers. At the same time, traditional seeds, which are less prone to pests and diseases, are lost over time or are not easily recovered.

134. The loss of ancestral lands and the undermining of indigenous cultures expose indigenous peoples to significant socio-economic vulnerabilities that challenge the very survival of their communities. Those vulnerabilities may reveal themselves as a loss of traditional knowledge, cultural diversity and biodiversity, further weakening the capacity of indigenous peoples for self-determination and survival. An adverse economic impact is seen in lost livelihoods and means of survival, poverty and increased dependence on State support. In mainstream society, indigenous peoples are often relegated to menial jobs since they often do not have the educational background, language skills or training necessary to compete. If they cannot find even menial jobs, they are marginalized and left in rural refuges or reserves. In

rural areas they also are the poorest peasants.[24] Social and demographic vulnerabilities include migration, often for economic reasons; the breakdown of intergenerational support; and the social disintegration that arises from alcohol and drug abuse, violent conflicts and abuses suffered by indigenous peoples.

135. Despite the paucity of recent and comprehensive data on social indicators related to indigenous peoples, scattered evidence points to the conclusion that, in many countries, indigenous peoples are among the poorest of the poor. Living conditions of indigenous peoples have often been found to be abominable and health problems severe. Furthermore, indigenous peoples lack access to essential social services like water, sanitation and electricity and have poorer quality housing as compared with non-indigenous populations.

Conclusion

136. Despite unprecedented material prosperity, improvements in methods of production and advances in information and communication technologies, the modern world continues to be afflicted with social problems, both old and new. Part of the problem is an old one: the unequal distribution of material wealth; and part of the problem is new, the issue of access to new technologies within and between countries of the world. Structural changes, often on a global scale, have led to some of the other social problems considered in the present chapter. The forces of globalization, manifested in increased flows of goods and services, information, cultural trends and people between the countries of the world, have not been matched by the policy measures and/or institutions needed to cope with the consequences. Those changes have added new dimensions to existing social problems, particularly with regard to employment.

137. As the global demand for labour in the formal economy remains weak — perpetuating high levels of unemployment, underemployment and low-productivity employment — income insecurity and vulnerability will continue to plague all social groups for the foreseeable future. Owing to preconceptions

---

[24] Xavier Albo, "Poverty, development and indigenous identity", in *Indigenous Development: Poverty, Democracy and Sustainability*, D. Iturralde and E. Krotz, editors (Washington, D.C., Inter-American Development Bank, 1996, No. IND96-102).

regarding their age, disability or cultural foundations, members of social groups are frequently relegated to the bottom of the hiring scale, making it more difficult for them to benefit from economic expansions and more likely that they will suffer when economies contract. One of the challenges to poverty reduction efforts is to ensure that opportunities for productive employment become more evenly spread throughout the population so that they reach the more disadvantaged and socially excluded groups. In the absence of such efforts, further integration and empowerment of economically and socially vulnerable populations is unlikely to occur in the short term.

II. Social ills

138. Although economic factors figure prominently among the causes of vulnerability, as explained in chapter I, many other factors often contribute to and reinforce economic disadvantage. Coping capacity is reduced, not only by a lack of financial assets and income, but also by limited access to health services and limited or no access to education. Health and education are therefore important contributors to and significant factors in determining earnings capacity and personal development.

The poor state of children's education and health

139. Health, education and social exposure are critical elements of a child's well-being. Furthermore, they are powerful determinants of a child's future, particularly of his/her development and behaviour during adolescence. It is therefore important to grasp the full significance of the vulnerabilities experienced by children because they can have a major influence on what happens to those children when they grow older and join the ranks of youth.

140. The education of children is a key factor in reducing the sources, manifestations and consequences of vulnerability, including poverty and child labour. Education is also a right, articulated in article 26 of the Universal Declaration of Human Rights, which recognizes the human value of education, and that education is indispensable in strengthening respect for human rights and fundamental freedoms. Thus, reducing vulnerabilities in one area is also related to reducing them in others: education is one of the key factors in reducing not only social and economic vulnerability, but also for reducing vulnerabilities related to human rights and to political and judicial systems.

141. Millions of children and youth under 18 worldwide are engaged in labour that hinders their education, development and future livelihoods. Many of them are engaged in the worst forms of child labour that cause irreversible physical and/or psychological damage, or that even threaten their lives, including forced and bonded labour, forced recruitment into armed conflict, prostitution and pornography, and other illicit activities. The International Labour Organization estimates that in 2000 an estimated 211 million children aged 5 to 14 were engaged in some form of economic activity.[25] Of those, 186 million[26] were engaged in child labour, including in its worst forms, to which the ILO member States, through agreed ILO conventions, have given priority for abolition. Of an estimated 141 million youth aged 15 to 17 engaged in economic activity, 59 million are engaged in child labour. When broken down by gender under the general classification of economic activity, girls and boys are involved equally up to the age of 14, while above that age the proportion of boys increases. For those engaged in what is considered to be child labour, boys' involvement is higher than that of girls for both the 5 to 14 and 15 to 17 age groups.[27]

142. Children who receive a primary education are already on the way to obtaining the tools and necessary foundation for reducing the potential for vulnerability as adults. Access to and completion of a primary education is the route to basic literacy and, of course, to a secondary education. Children of primary school age who do not go to school today are the young adult illiterates of tomorrow, whose life prospects, for employment and in general, are the bleakest of all. World leaders have recognized the importance of primary education by agreeing to the Millennium Development Goal targets on achievement of universal primary education and the elimination of gender disparity at all levels of education by 2015. Currently an estimated 113 million children of primary school age, of which 56 per cent are girls, are not enrolled

---

[25] According to the International Labour Organization, "economic activity" is a broad concept that encompasses most productive activities undertaken by children, whether for the market or not, paid or unpaid, for a few hours or full time, in a casual or regular basis, legal or illegal. It excludes schooling and chores undertaken in the child's own household. It is a statistical, but not a legal definition, and it is not the same as "child labour", referred to with regard to abolition.

[26] *A Future without Child Labour: Global Report under the Follow-up to the ILO Declaration on Fundamental Principles and Rights at Work*, Report of the Director-General to the International Labour Conference, ninetieth session, 2002 (Geneva, International Labour Office, 2002).

[27] Ibid.

Box 4
Assessing vulnerabilities: youth illiteracy

The lack of access to education constitutes one of the major dimensions of poverty and limits economic, social, cultural and political opportunities for poor people. Youth illiteracy remains alarmingly high in many regions, in particular among young women.

Regionally, the illiteracy rates for young women are the most severe in sub-Saharan Africa, where in many countries the proportion is over 40 per cent, and in some even over 70 per cent. Illiteracy rates for young men often exceed 30 per cent.

Source: UNESCO, Institute for Statistics, 2002.

---

in school.[28] Of those, 94 per cent are living in developing countries. Just over one third of the total are in sub-Saharan Africa, another one third in South and West Asia and 13 per cent in East Asia and the Pacific.

143. Not all children enrolled in primary school today will remain in school long enough to reach minimum levels of literacy and numeracy. Although illiteracy has decreased in all regions, during the period 1995 to 1999 in sub-Saharan Africa and South Asia, only 61 per cent of primary school entrants reached grade five, generally considered as the minimum required for basic literacy.[29] In many countries, children enrol in primary school at a late age. Educational systems that have high rates of enrolment in primary school at a higher age also tend to have high dropout rates prior to grade five. Leaving school before grade five and failing to attain minimum levels of literacy have a profound impact on the entry of children into adolescence and youth and on their subsequent ability to find decent employment. Although primary school enrolment has continuously increased over the past five decades, the number of illiterate young people has remained largely constant, mostly as a result of population growth.

144. In addition to the questions of increasing primary enrolment rates to achieve universal enrolment and retaining children in school through at least grade five,

there is the question of educational quality. Millions of children are taught by committed but untrained and underpaid teachers in sometimes overcrowded, unhealthy and poorly equipped classrooms. In some countries, the high number of children repeating grades, whether resulting from attendance or performance problems, is a serious drain on the capacity of educational systems. In addition, some countries do not have enough primary school teachers, particularly the least developed countries, where classes with 100 pupils are common. It has also been argued that in sub-Saharan Africa, where women represent less than half of the teaching staff, a strategy for facilitating girls' access to education would be to increase the proportion of women teachers, which would help girls to improve their learning process and lead to an improvement in women's participation in all economic and social sectors. Children, particularly in rural areas, have to walk many kilometres before reaching a school, making them vulnerable to various kinds of abuse by peers and adults.

145. Related to the issue of quality of education is the quality of pupils' health. There is evidence that children with poor health face greater learning challenges owing to illness, which causes absenteeism, and perhaps an inability to concentrate in classrooms. The implication is that they are likely to grow up to be poorly educated in addition to being in poor health. Such children can be expected to face problems later on, including the probability that they will have difficulty in finding decent-paying work and will therefore have lower earnings than their healthy counterparts. Therefore poor health in childhood can

---

[28] United Nations Educational, Scientific and Cultural Organization, *Education for all — Is the World on Track?*, EFA *Global Monitoring Report* (Paris, 2002).

[29] United Nations Children's Fund, *The State of the World's Children, 2003* (United Nations publication, E.03.XX.1), table 4.

have a significant impact on the child's educational attainment, which can in turn affect his or her future earning capacity as well as the ability to cope with future uncertainties.

146. Sources of vulnerability for children in terms of physical health and well-being begin before birth, as the health of an infant begins with the health of the mother. Poor maternal health and nutrition contribute to low birth weight in 20 million newborns each year — almost 20 per cent of all births.[30] Low birth-weight infants have a higher risk of dying before reaching their first birthday and are at greater risk for infection, malnutrition and long-term disabilities, including visual and hearing impairments, learning disabilities and mental retardation.

147. At least 30 to 40 per cent of infant deaths are the result of poor care during pregnancy and delivery. Those deaths could be avoided with improved maternal health, adequate nutrition and health care during pregnancy, and appropriate care during childbirth. The well-being of children is also linked to the literacy and education status of mothers: children of mothers with no education are more than twice as likely to die or be malnourished compared to children of mothers with a secondary or higher-level education.[31] Even though neonatal mortality has declined, the rates of decline have been much slower than those for infants and children below 5 years of age. Nevertheless, of the 8 million infants who die each year, possibly half die within the first month of life. That is largely a result of the slow progress achieved in maternal health.[32]

148. Malnutrition affects 150 million children under 5 years of age, or one third of all children below that age.[33] Although underweight prevalence declined from 32 per cent to 28 per cent in developing countries over

the past decade, with the most progress in East Asia and the Pacific, worldwide about 183 million children weigh less than they should for their age; some 67 million children are "wasted", that is, below the weight they should be for their height; and 226 million are stunted. Children in some regions are particularly vulnerable: half of all children in South Asia are underweight, and in sub-Saharan Africa, where one of every three children is underweight, the nutritional status of children is worsening. Being underweight and wasting are only the most obvious forms of malnutrition; micronutrient deficiencies affect approximately 2 billion people worldwide, and 250 million pre-school children are clinically deficient in vitamin A, essential to the functioning of the immune system.[34]

149. Disease affects malnourished children, who have lowered resistance to infection and are more likely to die from such common childhood ailments as diarrhoeal diseases and respiratory infections. For those who survive, frequent illness saps their nutritional status, locking them into a vicious cycle of recurring sickness, faltering growth and diminished learning ability. Nearly 12 million children under five die each year in developing countries, mainly from preventable causes, and over half of those deaths are either directly or indirectly attributable to malnutrition. Although global deaths of children under 5 years of age have fallen from 20 million to 12 million annually over the last four decades, during the same period deaths of children under age 5 in sub-Saharan Africa almost doubled, from 2.3 to 4.5 million per year. Five major yet preventable diseases — pneumonia, diarrhoea, malaria, measles and HIV/AIDS — account for about half of all childhood deaths. Other preventable diseases relate to the lack of access to safe drinking water and inadequate sanitation. More than one billion people cannot obtain safe drinking water, and more than two billion people lack access to adequate sanitation.[35]

150. Ironically, while malnutrition continues to be endemic in parts of South Asia and Africa, obesity is

[30] Safe Motherhood Inter-agency Group, *Safe Motherhood Fact Sheets*, available from http://www.safemotherhood.org/resources/publications.html

[31] UNICEF, *Progress since the World Summit for Children: A Statistical Review* (United Nations publication, Sales No. E.01.XX.20). Source data from over 35 Demographic and Health Surveys carried out between 1995 and 1999.

[32] World Health Organization, *Strategic Directions for Improving the Health and Development of Children and Adolescents* (WHO/FCH/CAH/02.21).

[33] "A world fit for children", final document of the special session on children, in *Official Records of the General Assembly, Twenty-seventh Special Session, Supplement*

No. 3 (A/S-27/19/Rev.1 and corrigenda), annex.

[34] Sustain, *Malnutrition Overview* (Washington, D.C., 2002), available from http://www.sustaintech.org/world.htm.

[35] "A world fit for children", final document of the special session on children, in *Official Records of the General Assembly, Twenty-seventh Special Session, Supplement No. 3* (A/S-27/19/Rev.1 and corrigenda), annex.

Box 5

Assessing vulnerabilities: malnutrition among children

Malnutrition among children, as measured by the proportion of children under the age of 5 who are underweight and underheight, is startling in many regions.

Malnutrition is most prevalent in the regions of sub-Saharan Africa, South Asia and East Asia and the Pacific, where in many countries over 40 per cent of the children are underweight or underheight.

Source: FAO, *State of Food Insecurity in the World, 2002* (Rome, 2002), and World Bank, *World Development Indicators, 2003* (Washington, D.C., 2003).

---

becoming a major health problem, not only in developed countries but increasingly in many developing countries as well. The number of obese children continues to grow, and chances that an overweight child will suffer lifelong weight problems are high. According to the World Health Organization (WHO), developing countries are seeing rapid increases in body mass indexes, a height/weight formula used to measure overweight and obesity, particularly among the young. WHO also estimates that worldwide some one billion people can be considered overweight, with 300 million people clinically obese.[36] The share of young people (children and youth) in the totals is unknown, but the long-term consequences for public health systems can be extensive and structural. In developing countries, there is the likelihood of new demands and an increased strain on public health services, as health-care systems will need to deal with both tropical and preventable diseases as well as with obesity-related illnesses, such as diabetes and cardiovascular disease, which typically require high-cost treatment.

151. One disease not clinically related to malnutrition or poor nutrition, but very much related to poverty, is HIV/AIDS. Roughly 16 per cent of all new HIV infections in 2001 were among children. About 800,000 infants were infected with HIV, mainly through mother-to-child transmission, in 2002. Largely as a result of the high infection rates among pregnant women in Africa, it appears that children are currently the fastest-growing age group among HIV infections: the total of 800,000 infections in 2002 contributed to a current total of 3 million infected children (table). Currently, some 1.8 million pregnant women are infected with HIV/AIDS, 1.5 million of whom are in sub-Saharan Africa. Mother-to-child transmission of the virus through pregnancy, labour, delivery or breastfeeding is responsible for over 90 per cent of the HIV infections in infants and children under the age of 15. HIV/AIDS has begun to undermine the years of steady progress in child survival. In the worst affected areas, the under-five mortality rate is expected to increase by over 100 per cent.[37]

---

[36] World Health Organization, *World Health Report, 2002: Reducing Risks, Promoting Healthy Life* (Geneva, 2002). See also Seth Mydans, "Clustering in cities, Asians are becoming obese", *New York Times* (13 March 2003).

[37] Joint United Nations Programme on HIV/AIDS, *Epidemic Update* (December, 2002); and World Health Organization, *World Health Report, 2002: Reducing Risks, Promoting Healthy Life* (Geneva, 2002).

Table
Children, youth and HIV/AIDS in 2002

(Millions)	Have been infected with HIV/AIDS	Currently living with HIV/AIDS	Newly infected in 2002	Died from HIV/AIDS in 2002
Adults	62	42.0	5.0	3.1
Youth (15-24)	22	12.0	2.4	1.5
Children	4-5	3.0	0.8	0.6

Source: UNAIDS, *Epidemic Update* (December, 2002); and Vivian Lopez, "HIV/AIDS and young people — a review of the state of the epidemic and its impact on world youth", paper presented at the Expert Group Meeting on Global Priorities for Youth, Helsinki, 6-10 October 2002. Figures in italics are estimates.

152. A second devastating effect of the HIV/AIDS pandemic on children is the emergence of a new group of children who are AIDS orphans. More than 11 million children currently under 15 have lost one or both parents to AIDS. That number is forecast to more than double by 2010. Before the onset of AIDS, about 2 per cent of all children in developing countries were orphans. By the end of 2002, in the 10 worst affected countries of Africa, more than 15 per cent of the children had become orphans.

153. The social and economic impacts of AIDS threaten the well-being and security of millions of children worldwide. As parents and other family members become ill, children take on greater responsibility for income generation, food production and care of family members. They face decreased access to adequate nutrition, basic health care, housing and clothing. Fewer families can afford to send their children to school, with young girls at particular risk of being denied an education first. Isolated from emotional connections with the family, some turn to risky sexual behaviour. While most of these children were born free of HIV, they become highly vulnerable to infection themselves.[38]

154. Health and education-related vulnerabilities experienced during childhood continue to have a strong bearing on adolescent development. Equally important is the fact that those vulnerabilities may also have implications for adolescents in terms of both their behaviour, particularly risk-taking and antisocial behaviours, and their perception of social reality.

Youth drug abuse and juvenile delinquency

155. Two significant sources and manifestations of social vulnerability and risk for youth are drug abuse and juvenile delinquency. Drug abuse is a source of vulnerability, in that it can lead to undesirable and negative consequences, such as early termination of education, unemployment or even HIV/AIDS from the use of unsterilized needles. However, it also is a consequence of vulnerability. Youth with emotionally unsupportive or troubled and unstable families or who feel unhappy and without hope as a result of their socio-economic status or perceived futures may turn to drugs to relieve stress and escape their current situation. Similarly, juvenile delinquency is a source of vulnerability and risk, particularly when it is related to the possibility of continuing on to serious criminal activity in adulthood, as well as a consequence of young people taking action as a response to other emotional and/or socio-economic vulnerabilities.

156. No comprehensive international comparative data are available on drug use by young people. Youth drug use in developing countries remains particularly elusive. However, according to the data that are available, alcohol, tobacco and cannabis are the substances most commonly used by young people

---

[38] United States Agency for International Development, UNICEF and UNAIDS, "Impacts on children, families, and communities", in *Children on the Brink, 2002: A Joint Report on Orphan Estimates and Program Strategies* (Washington, D.C., TvT Associates/The Synergy Project, 2002) available from http://www.unicef.org/publications/pub_children_on_the_brink_en.pdf.

around the world.[39] The first drugs used are usually tobacco and alcohol and, in some communities, inhalants. The greatest use of substances is generally found in the last two years of high school, continuing into early adulthood in most countries. In almost all regions, boys are more likely to use all substances than girls and are more likely to use them in risky ways. Rates of alcohol and tobacco use by students in Europe appear to be the highest in the world, while students in North America and Australia appear to have the highest rates of illicit drug use.

157. Urban youth tend to use substances to a greater extent than those in rural areas. Similarly, countries in social and political transition, such as those in Central and Eastern Europe, may have an environment that contributes to increased use of substances by young people. Tobacco and alcohol consumption has also been promoted through aggressive marketing campaigns reaching ever-increasing numbers of people worldwide despite efforts in some countries, including harsh health warnings, to curb marketing aimed at younger populations.

158. Young people use substances for many of the same reasons adults do, such as to relieve stress and heighten enjoyment, yet there are other reasons that are specifically related to adolescent development. Young people are at a stage in life where they desire and need to demonstrate independence from parental and societal authority, and take risks and satisfy their curiosity about new experiences while often being exposed to negative peer pressure. Many experiment with drugs; some go further and adopt risk-taking behaviours, such as drug and alcohol abuse, habitual use of tobacco or delinquency.

159. Although substance-use decisions also involve perceptions of risk by the individual, it has long been established that young people tend to ignore the long-term risks associated with substance use. Young people also tend to minimize the risks posed by their own substance use, with young men tending to do so more than young women. Young people almost everywhere generally tend to use substances to a greater extent and in riskier ways than older people.

160. Social vulnerability and exclusion have a direct influence on the risks of youth using and abusing drugs. Recent studies examining substance use patterns distinguish between mainstream youth and youth living in difficult circumstances with fewer opportunities and less support, including young people living in developing countries as well as those living out of the mainstream and experiencing social exclusion in developed countries. Substance use by those young people, often referred to as the "especially vulnerable", tends to be aimed more at relieving difficult circumstances, including physical or emotional pain, and at coping with such things as neglect, violence, physical or sexual abuse, homelessness and war, or with difficult economic circumstances, such as longer working hours and unemployment. In contrast, mainstream youth are more likely to use substances to enhance pleasure and as part of their leisure activities and culture. While there may be some overlap between the two, the issues and challenges can be quite different. Substance use and abuse by young people living in difficult circumstances strongly illustrates how drug abuse is also a consequence of social vulnerability.

161. Juvenile delinquency is another source and consequence of youth social vulnerability and risk and is often highly correlated with drugs and drug abuse. Juvenile delinquency encompasses a multitude of different violations of legal and social norms, ranging from minor offences to severe crimes committed by minors. Some types of juvenile delinquency are considered to be part of the process of maturation and growth and disappear as young people make the transition to adulthood. Many socially responsible adults committed some kind of petty offence during their adolescence. Arrests rates, mainly for petty offences, are typically highest among 15 to 19 year-olds.[40] However, at the other extreme, other juveniles create stable criminal groups with a corresponding subculture and begin to engage in the same activities as adult criminal groups.

162. The available data show that delinquency and crime are gender-specific, with males being more

---

[39] Unless otherwise indicated, data presented on drug use are from Gary Roberts, "Youth and drugs", paper presented at the Expert Group Meeting on Global Priorities for Youth, Helsinki, October 2002.

[40] Michael L. Benson, *Crime and the Life Course: An Introduction* (Los Angeles, California, Roxbury Publishing Company, 2002).

vulnerable and at risk than females.[41] The crime rates of male juvenile and male young adult offenders recorded by the police are more than double those of females. Young males are convicted six or seven times more often than young females. The number of male juvenile suspects per 100,000 per age group is more than six times the number of females, and in the case of young offenders it is even 12.5 times as many. Many possible reasons for those differences exist, including less social tolerance of behavioural deviations by girls than by boys, stronger family control over girls than over boys, and social and historical differences between the sexes with respect to violence, such that young men may use violence as a means to construct gender identity.

163. Juvenile crime has become a worldwide problem. During the 1990s, a majority of the regions of the world suffered from a rise in youth crime. Countries in transition have been particularly affected; since 1995, juvenile crime in a number of countries in transition has increased by more than 30 per cent. Juvenile crime levels in developed countries remain high, both by historical standards and in comparison to other countries. Delinquency is also a problem in developing countries, where juvenile delinquency and extreme juvenile problems occur at levels higher than in other countries, particularly in relation to street children, who have ruptured ties with their families and engage in various survival activities on the street.

164. Data from many countries also show that delinquency is largely a group phenomenon, for two thirds to three fourths of all juvenile offences are committed in groups. Group delinquency, in which the young people belonging to a particular group form and share a joint assumed identity, exhibits the characteristics of a subcultural group. The most extreme examples of this, and the most likely participants in group delinquent activities, are territorial gangs. According to statistical evidence, juvenile gangs commit three times more crimes than young people who are not gang members. Studies reveal that the most frequent offences committed by the gangs are fighting, street extortion and school violence; however, the appearance of juvenile street gangs is almost always also accompanied by drug trafficking.

Children and adolescents are more likely to be victims of juvenile crimes than other social groups: in general, the victims of juvenile crimes usually belong to the same age group as the perpetrators.

165. While economic factors, including high unemployment and poverty, may strongly influence youth delinquency, they are not always pivotal, and other social factors, such as cultural norms and values, family cohesion, peer-group influence and a supportive social environment also play a role. For example, in western societies, disinvestment of social capital in poor urban neighbourhoods may very well explain the increased occurrence of crimes by young people.[42] Urbanization may also play a role — urbanized societies have higher registered juvenile crime rates in comparison with countries with a strong rural lifestyle. One explanation is that urbanized societies may have less social control and social cohesion, whereas societies that are more rural are able to rely to a greater extent on family and community control to deal with antisocial behaviour.

166. The role of families and family life is clearly important: young people living in so-called dysfunctional families, characterized by conflict, inadequate parental control, weak ties with other members of the extended family and community, and premature autonomy, are closely associated with delinquency. As with drug use, children and young people in disadvantaged families with fewer opportunities for legitimate employment and who face either the risks or reality of social exclusion are overrepresented among juvenile offenders. If, in addition to living in a dysfunctional and disadvantaged family, a youth is also of an ethnic minority or from a migrant family, the level of vulnerability to delinquency can be even higher.

167. Other factors that can have an influence are the media, such as television violence and its popularization of violent heroes, low educational attainment, social exclusion, peer group pressure, the adoption of delinquent images and a delinquent identity by adolescents, and also the prospect of financial award from delinquent behaviour. For example, selling drugs is associated with financial reward, particularly in communities where there are few other, or otherwise

---

[41] Unless otherwise indicated, data on juvenile delinquency are from Alexander Salagaev, "Juvenile delinquency", paper presented at the Expert Group Meeting on Global Priorities for Youth, Helsinki, October 2002.

[42] See, for example, Benson, op. cit., chap. III, for an overview of John Hagan's theory of criminal capital and disinvestment.

low-paying, economic opportunities. However, the drug "business" is also associated with increases in the rate of violent and aggravated crimes, including by young people, thus leading to a perverse relationship in which drug abuse and juvenile delinquency are mutually reinforcing.

Health-related vulnerability of older persons' health

168. A major source of vulnerability for older persons is a lack of access to appropriate health care. Over the past two decades, changes in economic thinking and approaches have brought about a restructuring of social welfare policies, particularly in health care. In many countries, economic reforms have resulted in the diffusion of responsibility for the provision of health-care services and in the removal of health subsidies, which has increased the demands on household income. Many of the changes have had a wide impact on older persons in terms of affordability and access, particularly if discriminatory health-care rationing based on age is instituted. Whereas medical advances have extended lives and reduced disability, inequalities in longevity and health disparities within and between countries have widened. For a vast majority of people, including older persons, ill health is related to poverty, and health-care improvement in a country is related to its political economy and overall strategies of development.

169. Many factors affect the health of individuals as they get older and become exposed to increasing risk of illness and disability. Lifetime exposure to poverty means that many people reach old age already in chronic ill health, showing signs of poverty and disease before their sixtieth birthday. Chronic illnesses, including heart disease, cancer and mental disorders, are fast becoming the world's leading causes of death and disability. Non-communicable diseases now account for 59 per cent of all deaths globally, which means that developing countries have a double burden of disease: rapid growth of non-communicable diseases at the same time that they are struggling with malnutrition and infectious diseases such as HIV/AIDS, malaria and tuberculosis. Chronic diseases, which increase dramatically at the older ages, are significant and costly causes of disability. It is especially true for older women who, because of greater longevity, have higher incidences of

impairment and disability, but whose vulnerability to disability is also generated by gender inequalities over the life course and a lack of understanding of their physical, mental-health and post-menopausal needs.

170. Older ethnic minorities tend to suffer greater discrimination and disadvantage at every level, including health. Whereas the health profile of those groups is comparable to the majority older population at the lowest socio-economic strata, their constant existence on the margins points to greater and more acute vulnerability. Further, in spite of having a poorer health profile, older minorities are frequently found to be isolated from mainstream health and social care services. A number of reasons can be cited for their situation: lack of awareness of services, resulting in part from ineffective dissemination of information and outreach by mainstream organizations; language barriers, including illiteracy; user fees and issues of transport; and problems of perception and mistrust between service providers and the older persons. The issue of perception is of particular importance and can impact all the other issues. Older minorities feel that providers do not allocate culturally appropriate care that may address dietary, religious and linguistic differences. In addition, when outreach attempts are made, they are often based on stereotypical assumptions about the minority group.[43]

171. Until recently the prevalence of HIV/AIDS among and its effects on older persons had been largely ignored owing to the unavailability of data, which excludes the effect of the pandemic on the older population in many parts of the world, including sub-Saharan Africa, where the decimation of the population from AIDS is most severe. In Western Europe, nearly 10 per cent of the new infections declared between January 1997 and June 2000 were among persons over 50. In the United States of America, 10 per cent of all reported cases occur among people over 50, and over half are of African-American and Hispanic origin, indicating greater risks among minority groups. Many of the older infected persons may have had the virus for years before being tested, at which time the infection may be in its most advanced stages. Further,

---

[43] "Minority ethnic elder care: a synopsis of country profiles" (Leeds, United Kingdom, Policy Research Institute on Ageing and Ethnicity [PRIAE], 2002), prepared under the three-year Minority Ethnic-Elder Care research programme, a European Commission Fifth Framework Programme.

age accelerates the progress of HIV to AIDS, and age-related conditions, such as osteoporosis, increase the risk of severe complications.[44]

172. The consequences of HIV/AIDS extend far beyond the disease itself. As mentioned above, AIDS has resulted in growing numbers of orphans around the world. Older persons, mostly women, are not only taking on the care of children who have been orphaned by the disease, but are also suffering the magnitude and complexity of the consequences: orphaned children are more likely to have poorer nutrition, be underweight, drop out of school, and face depression and psychological problems. If they do not have a grandparent to care for them, they are more likely to live on the streets, be exploited because they are forced to work or sell their bodies as their only asset.[45] The burden of caring for the children is extraordinary, especially when it is put in the context of local environments that are already ravaged by conflict, famine, displacement and conditions of extreme poverty. Furthermore, many older persons who take on such new responsibilities are already in mourning and deprived of the support from their adult children that they had expected in their old age. Their own resources are seriously depleted at the same time that they are called on to help others possibly worse off than they.

173. In a recent case study on the effect of HIV/AIDS on older persons, findings suggested that the loss of remittances and other economic support, the lack of food and clothing, the high cost of medical fees during illness, and the inability to pay school fees for orphans affected the ability of older persons to provide care. Older persons were under serious physical and emotional stress, and cases of physical violence, stigma and abuse resulting from witchcraft accusations were prevalent. Moreover, older persons infected with the disease experienced limited access to health services owing to the high cost of care, transport difficulties, the stigma of the disease and the attitudes of health workers.[46]

174. At a wider level, AIDS is causing life expectancy to decline. In Southern Africa alone it has fallen from over 60 years to under 50, and it is expected to fall further. Moreover, the movement of HIV/AIDS eastward into Asia, combined with the rapid growth of death rates from tuberculosis and malaria, will result in a continued reduction of life expectancy and an increase in the vulnerability of and burden on older persons, with far-reaching health, economic and psychosocial impacts.

Migrant health and social protection

175. Three elements can be identified as the source of health-related vulnerability among migrants. First, there is evidence that their health risks are compounded by discrimination and restricted access to health information, health promotion, health services and health insurance. Second, migrants as a group disproportionally suffer from high exposure to occupational and environmental hazards. Third, migrants are at greater risk because some of their specific health needs are ignored or not well understood and therefore are not adequately addressed.

176. Migrant health is an area of intense debate. Concerns with pre-existing and untreated conditions such as infectious and communicable diseases have long been a priority for health authorities, since migrants pose potential sanitary threats to host populations. A few years ago, considerable public and media attention was devoted to the association between migrants and HIV/AIDS. The focus has now switched to the health threat posed by undocumented migrants. There is also speculation on whether a significant number of migrants may be motivated by the health-care entitlements in host countries that provide them with treatment not available or affordable in their country of origin. It is argued that the provision of health care to migrants puts additional financial stress on already overstretched and underperforming public health systems. In addition, the use of a health condition in court as a ground to challenge expulsion orders in several countries has caused further uneasiness on the part of public authorities. It has also undermined the case for a legally binding recognition of health as a human right. So far, although migrants

44 UNAIDS and World Health Organization, "HIV/AIDS and older people", in *Building a Society for All Ages, Second World Assembly on Ageing, Madrid, Spain, 8-12 April 2002* (DPI/2264), available from http://www.un.org/ageing/prkit/hivaids.htm.
45 Alan Whiteside, "Future imperfect: the AIDS epidemic in the twenty-first century", inaugural lecture, University of Natal, Durban, South Africa, 5 December 2002.
46 World Health Organization, *Impact of AIDS on Older People in Africa: Zimbabwe Case Study* (WHO/NMH/NPH/ALC/02.12).

have argued that expulsion should not be enforced when there are serious, including life-threatening, health conditions and a need for medical treatments that might not be available in the migrant's country of origin, all courts have rebutted their claims.

177. Migrant health poses a triple challenge by raising fundamental questions of social equity, public health and human rights. Unfortunately, the current controversial context makes it difficult to reduce their health-related vulnerability despite ample evidence of their plight. For example, in Europe, occupational accident rates are, on average, twice as high for migrant workers than for native workers. In both developed and developing countries, many migrant agricultural workers display pathologies related to exposure to toxic pesticides. The large majority of those migrants do not have medical coverage or access to health services.

178. Work carried out by the World Health Organization and the World Bank on mental health has found that immigrants and refugees are among the groups that are disproportionately affected. Although knowledge of the mental health of migrant populations remains fairly limited, there is enough evidence to suggest that severe psychological stress due to uprooting, disruption of family life and a hostile social environment is common. Unfortunately, a large number of migrants have no or little access to mental health care, either because they are excluded from existing service arrangements or because there is no provision for mental health care, a situation that prevails in more than 40 per cent of countries.

179. Trafficking and smuggling expose migrants to additional health hazards, including dangerous travel conditions, violence and abuse, and unsafe working environments. Those who are trafficked for work in the sex industry face increased risks of sexually transmitted diseases. At the same time, the fear of deportation and the absence of medical insurance make them unlikely to seek medical care.

180. Migrants who live in societies that have extensive social protections systems do benefit from them. However, owing to existing institutional arrangements and piecemeal adaptation to the changing nature of migration flows, the social protection of migrants and their access to social programmes are fragmented, partial and inadequate. The inadequacy of coverage also reflects a lack of concern for the social needs of migrants. Nevertheless, the availability of welfare benefits to migrants has given rise to a heated debate between those who support the right of migrants to comprehensive social benefits and those for whom the debate on immigration policy centres on the trade-off between the economic benefits of immigration and social redistribution.

181. At a basic level, migrants' entitlement to social protection depends on whether they live in a country where welfare benefits are provided primarily as a result of being employed and having contributed to the social insurance system — such as in the labour-importing countries of Western Europe — or in a country where benefits are granted on the basis of residence — such as the traditional countries of immigration (Australia, Canada, New Zealand and the United States), the Scandinavian countries or the United Kingdom of Great Britain and Northern Ireland. In labour-importing countries, social benefits depend largely on the migrant's specific status — for example, primary visa holder, dependant or refugee — and time requirements. As welfare provisions are often contained in bilateral treaties, the migrant's country of origin also matters.

182. In most cases, migrants do not qualify for welfare benefits — beside health care — during their first year of residence. However, in a few countries, denial of social benefits may last longer, up to several years. Claiming social benefits may jeopardize a migrant's rights and that of his or her family to remain in the host country if he or she does not meet time requirements. Most importantly, residency requirements deny many migrants social benefits when joined by their families, namely at a time of great need.

183. In many countries, in particular in federal States, responsibility for social assistance programmes has been devolved to subnational authorities, increasing the complexity and the diversity of situations faced by migrants. Such differences make the availability of social provisions to migrants unequal both within and between host countries.

184. While health care is available to all migrants, including undocumented migrants on an emergency basis, the scope and quality of health services to which they have access vary greatly. However, there is evidence that migrants may sometimes be reluctant to assert their rights and do not avail themselves of the health services they are entitled to, for reasons ranging

from a lack of information to cultural gaps and various forms of discrimination. For unemployment benefits, social assistance and public housing, eligibility criteria are much more restrictive and often apply only to long-term residents. In a significant number of countries, non-nationals are excluded from certain benefits.

185. The non-portability of retirement benefits is increasingly attracting attention as an issue of equity. Despite many signed bilateral agreements, a large number of migrants, in particular from developing countries, fall outside those agreements and cannot receive pension benefits if they decide to leave the host country. The issue of the non-portability of benefits has gained additional momentum following the surge in the international recruitment and mobility of skilled workers.

186. The social protection of migrants is a question that lies at the core of the migration debate. It has been contended that the open welfare state offers a strong motivation for people with a low level of human capital to migrate. Whether there is an economic case or not, the controversy over the social protection of migrants is one of the issues that feeds anti-immigrant feelings.

Inadequate accessibility: a disability perspective

187. Every child is unique and has a fundamental right to education. However, in developing countries only a small minority of disabled children are in school, falling below 10 per cent in Asia and the Pacific.[47] When denied the basic right of education, disabled people become severely restricted in terms of their economic, social and political opportunities as well as the prospects for their personal development. Without an education it is more difficult to secure a job, particularly one that pays a decent wage, participate actively and fully in the community and have a meaningful voice in policy making, especially with regard to issues that directly concern the affected population.

188. Children and youth with disabilities face a host of barriers to education, starting with an inaccessible school environment. In most cases, the lack of proper teacher training and appropriate teaching materials and methods makes it unlikely that their special needs will be addressed in a timely fashion. Negative attitudes and exclusionary policies and practices towards children with disabilities as well as a lack of support systems for teachers further undermine the schooling options of children with disabilities. The problem is particularly severe in rural areas, as special education schools are located mainly in urban areas.

189. Given the dynamics of disability and health, access to adequate health-care services is essential for the promotion of independent living for the disabled. Health services play a critical role in the prevention, diagnosis and treatment of illnesses and conditions that can cause physical, psychological and intellectual impairments. However, for the majority of persons with disabilities living in developing countries, as well as for a significant minority living in industrialized countries, poverty precludes access to those vital services, either because health-care facilities and practitioners are not sufficiently available or because there are not enough funds to purchase needed medications and devices. Not only are there too few orthopaedic surgeons, the number of medical rehabilitation centres to help people adapt to disabling conditions is insufficient to meet the demand, and many more appliances such as orthotics, prostheses, hearing aids and wheelchairs are needed to improve daily functioning.

190. Independent living implies integrating the disabled into the general community, rather than placing them in exclusionary institutions or relegating them into "colonies" of disabled. Community-based rehabilitation programmes, which are in the process of becoming fairly well established in industrialized countries but remain rare in developing countries, tend to be part and parcel of independent living strategies. The intention of the programmes is to lower the costs and increase the effectiveness of disability services by replacing more costly, segregated, medically based institutional approaches with more cost-effective and responsive approaches intended to empower and support disabled persons and their families.[48]

---

[47] United Nations, Economic and Social Commission for Asia and the Pacific, *Asian and Pacific Decade of Disabled Persons*, 1993-2002, available from http://www.unescap.org/Decade.

[48] Robert L. Metts, "Disability issues, trends and recommendations for the World Bank", Social Protection Discussion Paper No. 0007 (Washington, D.C., World Bank, 2000).

191. The potential for enhancing the possibility of persons with disabilities to carry on independent lives within the community rests on the adoption of inclusive technologies and universal design in buildings, public facilities, communications systems and housing. Inclusive technical devices, such as wheelchairs, crutches, sign language translation, Braille machines, adaptive keyboards, and audio cassettes can significantly improve mobility and communication for the disabled. Likewise, adopting the principles of universal design can greatly facilitate the physical accessibility of schools, training centres, workshops, offices, public buildings and residences.[49] If those accommodations are made, disabled people will have greater ease of access to education, employment and social, political and cultural opportunities, all of which can improve their well-being and that of the communities in which they live.

Threats to the well-being of indigenous peoples

192. The overall well-being of indigenous peoples is threatened in a number of different ways. One major source of vulnerability is the risk of disintegration of the social structure that is crucial to their survival. Other sources of vulnerability, many of which are directly related to their social structure, include health problems; a lack of education and a lack of access to education; migration; armed conflict; loss of lands; and violence, exploitation and abuse.

193. The health of indigenous peoples is closely related to their lands. The appropriation of ancestral lands, environmental degradation and dwindling natural resources compromise agricultural livelihoods, the supply of food specific to their diets and the sources of their traditional medicines. Furthermore, indigenous peoples have been exposed to diseases that were once those of "outsiders"; the incidence of such illnesses as AIDS and cancer from radioactive pollutants, against which traditional medicine is not effective, has been on the rise among indigenous peoples.

194. In the area of education, indigenous peoples face discrimination in two spheres. First, they often lack access to educational facilities. Second, educational curricula seldom take into account the special characteristics of indigenous peoples. Thus, indigenous children often drop out of school, while those that do continue often face discrimination in gaining access to institutions of higher education.[50] Furthermore, compared to boys, indigenous girls are less likely to attend school, and fewer indigenous children attend school as compared with other children. As a result, the lowest literacy rates are often observed among indigenous women.

195. The opening of indigenous territories has led to the migration of indigenous youth to urban centres, leaving older members of the community in traditional settlements or at relocation sites. Urban migration erodes the intergenerational support that has sustained indigenous peoples over many years and severs ties to traditional territories. Older indigenous peoples, left on their own in less desirable physical environments, become victims of abuse and maltreatment, hunger and suicide.[51] The departure of the younger members results in higher dependency ratios within indigenous communities and, unless reversed, eventually leads to the extinction of those communities. There outmigration of indigenous women seeking work in other countries as domestic helpers has also increased.[52] While their remittances help indigenous communities financially, lasting outmigration also leads to the further breakdown of families and social values.

196. Increased military actions to combat drug cartels and armed insurgency, as well as the presence of

---

[49] See "Disability and poverty reduction strategies: how to ensure that access of persons with disabilities to decent and productive work is part of the PRSP process", discussion paper, InFocus Programme on Skills, Knowledge and Employability (Geneva, International Labour Organization, Disability Programme, 2002), para. 36.

[50] Chandra Roy, "Racial discrimination against indigenous peoples: a global perspective", *Indigenous Affairs*, No. 1 (2001).

[51] "Human rights of indigenous peoples: indigenous peoples and their relationship to land", final working paper prepared by the Special Rapporteur to the Commission on Human Rights (E/CN.4/Sub.2/2000/25).

[52] Victoria Tauli-Corpuz, *The Resistance of the Indigenous Peoples of Asia against Racism and Racial Discrimination* (Baguio City, Philippines, Indigenous Peoples' International Centre for Policy Research and Education, n.d.), available from http://www.tebtebba.org/tebtebba_files/ipr/racism.htm (accessed 4 November 2002).

paramilitary forces, have hastened the social disintegration of indigenous peoples' communities and have forced thousands of them off their lands, converting them into refugees.[53] The problem becomes even more difficult for indigenous communities located along the borders of several nation States where police protection is not effective.

197. Other conflicts exist between indigenous peoples and members of modern society coexisting on adjacent lands, stemming from differences in their concepts of land rights. Violent means have sometimes been used to evict indigenous peoples from their lands. Other human rights violations against indigenous peoples include assassinations, forced disappearances, compulsory relocation and destruction of villages and communities.[54] Missionary work of followers of institutionalized religions and the subsequent conversions of some members of indigenous communities have also led to conflicts within those communities and the rejection by some members of their indigenous cultures.

198. Another source of vulnerability is exploitation and abuse. Displaced women possessing only farming skills become easy prey to prostitution rings. In areas where land has been expropriated for logging, indigenous women may be forced into prostitution only to be left behind when the logging operations are completed.

199. Oppression and alienation from their own traditions has had serious sociocultural, psychological and emotional effects on indigenous peoples. This is manifested in a very high incidence of domestic abuse and violence, alcoholism and suicide in indigenous peoples' households, particularly in urban settings. "Over-policing" has also resulted in the overrepresentation of indigenous peoples in custody, with high levels of youth institutionalized and detained.[55] A high incidence of mental health problems has also been observed among indigenous children

taken from their families and placed as servants in non-indigenous homes.

200. The sources of vulnerability and problems mentioned above are exacerbated by indigenous peoples' isolation. They usually live in remote areas where access to health, education, housing and refugee services is limited. Indigenous peoples often have limited resources to protect themselves from violence or to punish perpetrators when formal justice and criminal justice systems are located in faraway urban areas.

Conclusion

201. Traditionally, the public sector provides basic social services, including education, health care and social assistance and social protection to ensure equal access and protect the basic needs of individuals, families and communities. Those services form an integral part of the capacity to cope with the effect of social risks. Unfortunately, fewer and fewer resources are available for such purposes in the current environment of public sector retrenchment in both developed and developing countries. As a result, there is a general trend towards reductions in public provisions while alternative methods of delivering basic services have fallen short of expectations in terms of universal access. The situation has further weakened coping capacity, especially among disadvantaged and vulnerable populations.

202. The disintegration of social infrastructure in the areas of education, health care and administration/governance, and the weakening of social institutions have put large segments of the population at risk for disease, lawlessness and ignorance, all of which contribute to increasing vulnerability.

203. Furthermore, the demographic transition brings with it such social concerns as older persons' health, which is becoming an issue for more people in more countries as population ageing occurs. All the while, precious resources are spent fighting expensive (both in money and human lives) wars instead of addressing social ills and the special needs of large segments of the population in some of the world's poorest countries. For some, they are trapped in a vicious cycle: poverty and unmet social challenges — violent conflict — deepening social division and poverty.

53 "Briefing notes", *World News*, 6 February 2001.
54 "Indigenous issues: human rights and indigenous issues", report of the Special Rapporteur on the situation of human rights and fundamental freedoms of indigenous peoples (E/CN.4/2002/97).
55 Aboriginal and Torres Strait Islander Social Justice Commissioner, *Social Justice Report, 1997* (Sydney, Australian Human Rights and Equal Opportunity Commission, 1997), available from http://www.humanrights.gov.au. Path: publications.

204. The challenges posed by the social ills analysed in the present chapter are great for both national Governments and the international community. Commitment and cooperation are needed at the national and international levels to address those issues.

III. Sociocultural biases and discrimination

205. The presence and persistence of sociocultural biases and discriminatory attitudes and practices can be readily identified as major contributors to vulnerability. Bias and discrimination are in a sense acts of social exclusion, as they prevent the groups that are the victims of those acts from fully participating in and benefiting from the wealth, power, knowledge and decision-making capacities of the larger society. At their worst, socio-economic biases and discrimination can produce feelings of disempowerment, hopelessness and despair for the future, further exacerbating vulnerability among the excluded groups. The inability to provide input to important policy decisions leaves them powerless and voiceless, resulting in their legitimate interests not being protected. Consequently, national policies and development programmes do not necessarily benefit those that are disenfranchised. Still, worse, their interests may even be sacrificed in the pursuit of such policies and programmes. As a result, social groups, households and individuals subject to such misperception and discrimination experience greater vulnerability to social exclusion.

206. The following are presented below as illustrations of the negative effects of bias and discrimination: the images and misperceptions of older persons; the vulnerabilities experienced by migrants; discrimination against the disabled; groups particularly at risk in situations of conflict; and the lack of respect for traditional knowledge and cultures of indigenous persons.

Images and misperceptions of older persons

207. On one level, perceptions of older persons follow the trajectory of a society's culture, religion, language, history and level of development. On another, they follow social conventions that adhere to established precedents and, once rooted, are difficult to alter. The social convention of classifying people on the basis of their age has enduring consequences that can create significant barriers to access and participation.

208. The contributions that older persons make to their families and communities are immense, but such contributions are easy to miss and are therefore overlooked in development strategies. Older persons are critical and active partners in families and societies through the care they provide to family members who might otherwise require more formal treatment; through the care and education they provide to children whose parents cannot afford childcare or who migrate elsewhere for work; through the countless other forms of volunteer work that they perform in communities and institutions everywhere; and through their help in conflict resolution and the rebuilding of communities following emergencies. In addition, older persons possess traditional knowledge and overall survival strategies accumulated over a lifetime of experience.

209. Paradoxically, however, older persons are cast in distorted images that inflate their physical and mental deterioration and dependence. The outcome is an anachronistic message that, on the broader level, colours an entire phase of life. It obscures older persons' contributions and generates ageism, discrimination and exclusion and, ultimately, contributes to a loss of rights in the social, economic and political spheres. Routine media misrepresentation that idolizes youth and views ageing as a time of incapacity and stagnation is particularly damaging to older persons, who already suffer greater exclusion, especially in an era of rapid technological change in which authority is often passed to younger members of society. Significantly, such images are not lost on centres of influence and power, such as employers, donors and policy makers — decision makers who can have an impact on older persons' access to structures and resources and therefore mitigate or increase vulnerability.

210. Globalization of the media has contributed to spreading ageism to societies in which it was traditionally unknown. The forces of globalization that have ushered in consumerism and individualism in developing countries have compounded the devaluation of the status of older persons, encouraging the view that they are burdens and a financial drain. The effects are becoming visible far beyond the local level, with a lack of opportunities for older persons, combined with the absence of economic assets and added responsibilities owing to the outmigration of younger adults, conspiring to force on older persons into greater economic and social dependence.

211. Negative self-image is inextricably bound up with stereotypes and is another factor that leads to social exclusion. Older persons with strong tendencies towards a negative self-image are also those who are in the greatest need of support. Those in poverty and conflict show a marked decline in self-esteem as they age and tend to share a view of ageing as a time of worthlessness, incapacity and loss of status that leads to dependence. For many, fears and self-doubt accumulate to such an extent that what is feared — exclusion and greater physical and economic dependence — becomes more likely. Low self-esteem becomes a risk in itself and helps to foster an image of a population with whom no one, including older persons themselves, wants to identify.

212. The perpetuation of misperceptions of ageing has a political impact as well. The expression "intergenerational conflict", which has appeared in the public discourse, suggests that, if steps are not taken, individual old-age pension and health-care security, or worse, national or even global financial stability, may be threatened with disruption. Such messages suggest a need to assign responsibility and ultimately serve as a pretext for cutting back on old-age provisions. Perceptions that an ageing society will deepen social conflict, however, are not so rooted in prejudices as to hold any particular age group responsible. Rather, social, economic and politically uncertain environments, with the support of the media, are shaping attitudes about society's unpreparedness to adjust to a changed demographic structure that has no precedent and therefore no previous basis from which to proceed.

213. Women and men move through the ageing process in different ways and encounter different obstacles and relative disadvantages en route. For women, balancing work and family responsibilities can be all-consuming. Their role as principal caregiver in the family often lingers into old age, when they care for their spouses and/or, in areas ravaged by poverty and disease, including HIV/AIDS, for their grandchildren and other family members who are orphaned or sick.

214. The feminization of poverty is found in all regions and particularly affects older women. It is linked to a lifetime of lower pay and interrupted employment histories; possibly heavy or hazardous work; lack of access to decision-making processes, education and resources, including credit and land ownership; and lack of established inheritance rights. Since older women are less likely to have paid work, they are less likely to be eligible for pensions. And when they are eligible, older women are more likely to receive lower pensions owing to their lower pay and work histories.

215. As a result of their longer life expectancy, older women are more likely than men to be widowed, isolated or even destitute in the last years of their lives. In situations of armed conflict or other disasters, informal support systems often vanish through death, disappearance or forced migration. In many developing countries the patriarchal customary, religious and inheritance laws leave older widows few options, if any, to escape situations of exploitation or discrimination. Gender bias is further reinforced through the legal system. When justice is sought, few cases proceed successfully through the courts; perpetrators go unpunished and others remain undeterred or undetected.[56]

216. In countries with economies in transition, the disintegration of social security and the dismantling of the welfare state have produced a subclass of impoverished older widows. Many have lost property rights and basic assistance and have become part of a tragic but increasingly common sight: the "street elderly". Even in developed countries, where legal protection is more inclusive, widows experience marginalization and the loss of social and economic status.[57]

217. Illiteracy rates for older women remain high in many parts of the world. Two thirds of the 862 million illiterate adults in the world are women.[58] The situation is particularly acute in South Asia and parts of Africa, where the rates can surpass 80 per cent. One of the devastating effects is to leave entire communities vulnerable, leading to apathy towards an alarming level of inequality and limiting the extent to which successive generations, particularly daughters, can realize their own human potential.

218. Owing to the traditional roles and status bestowed upon men as economic providers, older men are particularly affected when they are abruptly retired

56 "Widowhood: invisible women, secluded or excluded", *Women 2000* (December 2001).

57 Ibid.

58 UNESCO, *Education for All — Is the World on Track?*, EFA *Global Monitoring Report* (Paris, 2002).

from the workforce or when they find themselves unable to earn an income as a result of economic downturns and restructuring in the labour market. The effect of such events has been demonstrated in some countries with economies in transition where mortality rates have risen in the working age population and life expectancy trends among males have reversed course.

219. Since the break-up of the Soviet Union, a number of countries in transition have been plagued by long-term crises and dramatic increases in social stratification. Numerous indicators have been cited, ranging from rising rates of disease, alcohol consumption and accidents to homicides and suicides. Sources of the rising rates include the post-Soviet collapse in social protection and medical care, environmental pollution, stress associated with change, high unemployment, and the dramatic increase in poverty and income disparities. Although life expectancy has been experiencing slight increases since 1995, the mortality crisis is alarming. It has put a population that is not yet old at risk of ageing in even poorer health as they become an impoverished generation of "pensioners" who are considered today to be one of the most vulnerable groups in Eastern Europe.

220. In some countries in Latin America and the Caribbean, frail older men are considered particularly vulnerable to abandonment. For many of them, after they leave the labour market, their co-residence with their family falls off sharply and along with it material support. Although older women are seen as relatively desirable household members, given their well-established domestic roles, the male breadwinner who tended to neglect kinship and domestic matters during his working years finds, as a result, that his status and quality of family relations are seriously reduced in later life.[59]

221. Older persons are often viewed as frail, passive and economically non-productive, a misperception that is even spreading to societies where respect for the aged used to be the norm. That view has significant consequences for the well-being of older persons. It reinforces the tendency to exclude older persons from

decision-making in the social, economic and political spheres. It also forms the basis on which employment opportunities are denied to older persons. Older persons, and older women in particular, living in developing and transition economies face even greater difficulties. Economic as well as cultural changes taking place in those countries often have many negative implications for older persons, including more negative attitudes towards them and non-existent or collapsing old-age social protection. Women encounter additional hardships owing to discriminatory inheritance laws and their longer life expectancy. Leadership in public policy, especially in the media, is needed to dispel existing mistaken beliefs with regard to older persons. More importantly, appropriate public policy in areas of justice, pension reform and social protection is required, in addition to public education, in order to combat ageism and its harmful consequences.

Migrants' vulnerabilities

222. Migration is a pervasive issue that has a bearing on the economy, the social fabric and the political life of many countries. Viewpoints on migration are polarized to the degree that it is difficult to hold a rational debate on the issue. Against such a background of contention, the human dimension of international migration has often been missing from the policy agenda, and many migrants have increasingly found themselves vulnerable.

223. First, in the course of the migration process, individuals lose the security of essential family-, community- and nation-based support structures, including traditional institutions that regulate power, decision-making and protection, while at the same time they are exposed to a host of hazards for which they are largely unprepared. To a significant extent, the vulnerability of migrants stems from the nature of the immigration process, which remains, in much of the world — apart from a handful of traditional countries of immigration — long, challenging and poorly organized. During the course of the immigration process, migrants often receive little assistance from the host country and end up relying on immigrant communities and immigration networks of questionable legitimacy. In trying to circumvent admissions delays and restrictions, an increasing number of migrants are putting themselves at risk by electing to be smuggled

---

[59] Economic Commission for Latin America and the Caribbean, expert group meeting on social support networks for senior citizens: the role of the State, the family and the community (in Spanish), 9-12 December 2002.

into destination countries. Migration under such conditions carries with it the risk of possible abuse by smugglers, the legal consequences associated with being an illegal alien and other difficulties.

224. Secondly, migration by its very nature entails the deprivation of some rights. For example, in host countries with comprehensive coverage for citizens migrants do not receive the same rights to social protection and social services as nationals. Non-nationals do not have complete rights as nationals do. States lawfully grant privileges and protections to their nationals, including access to social services that are exclusionary of non-nationals. As a consequence, many migrants are deprived of or have limited social protection (for example, health, unemployment or pension benefits). In addition, the rights of migrants are often restricted in terms of employment, professional and geographical mobility, and family life. At the same time, evidence of growing problems with violations of migrants' rights, including basic human rights, has been met with limited concern.

225. Thirdly, migration has proven to be disruptive of the social cohesion of both displaced communities and host societies. Displacement eventually challenges traditional gender and generational roles. In host societies, particularly in Europe, migration has contributed to social polarization and has been a key factor in generating a feeling of social and political exclusion in poor, working-class communities. Increased stigmatization and marginalization of migrants have been observed, raising concern as to the potential for the social integration and mobility of immigrants. Furthermore, the enforcement of rights legally accorded to migrants is not a high priority on national agendas when in many countries an atmosphere of increasing xenophobia, stigmatization and racism prevails.

226. Finally, migration-related vulnerability is essentially of a political nature. While the process and social dynamics of migration and the status of migrants are potential sources of vulnerability, the failure of Governments to develop and implement policies that acknowledge and comprehensively address the large array of issues associated with modern migration, including responding to the specific needs of migrants and protecting their rights, is mainly responsible for migrants' vulnerability. The status of migrants as a largely voiceless group with no political leverage has certainly contributed to the situation.

Discrimination against the disabled

227. Persons with disabilities are often excluded from the mainstream of society and denied their human rights.[60] Both de jure and de facto discrimination against persons with disabilities have a long history and take various forms. They range from overt discrimination, such as the denial of educational opportunities, to more subtle forms of discrimination, such as segregation and isolation resulting from the imposition of physical and social barriers. The effects of disability-based discrimination have been particularly severe in such areas as education, employment, housing, transportation, cultural life and access to public places and services. Discrimination may result from exclusion, restriction or preference, or from denial of reasonable accommodation on the basis of disablement, which effectively nullifies or impairs the recognition, enjoyment or exercise of the rights of persons with disabilities.

228. Despite some progress in terms of legislation, such violations of the human rights of persons with disabilities have not been systematically addressed in society. Often, disability legislation and policies are based on the assumption that persons with disabilities are simply not able to exercise the same rights as non-disabled persons. Consequently, the situation of persons with disabilities is often addressed in terms of rehabilitation and social services. In many countries, existing provisions do not provide for the rights of disabled persons in all their aspects — that is, political, civil, economic, social and cultural rights — on an equal basis with persons without disabilities. Furthermore, anti-discrimination laws often have weak enforcement mechanisms, thereby denying opportunities for persons with disabilities to participate on an equal basis in social life and development.

229. Certain cultural and social barriers such as systematic institutionalization, regardless of the type and level of disability, have also served to deter the full participation of persons with disabilities. Discriminatory practices against persons with disabilities may thus be the result of social and cultural norms that have been institutionalized by law. In such a context, discrimination towards people that have an impairment is likely to continue until appropriate policy actions are taken to address and improve the

---

[60] *Disabled Persons Bulletin*, No. 2, 1998.

social and cultural norms that may perpetuate erroneous and inappropriate myths about disability.

230. To a great extent, the vulnerability of persons with disabilities arises from concrete forms of discrimination, such as the architectural barriers inherent in many buildings, forms of transportation and communication, and from a dramatic lack of employment opportunities. Nevertheless, access to rehabilitation services remains a critical component of the effort to promote social inclusion of the disabled. According to the World Health Organization, at most only 5 per cent of the disabled in developing countries have access to rehabilitation services.[61] Given the fact that at least 7 of 10 disabled people live in developing countries, the limited reach of rehabilitation services is evident.

231. Discrimination is a heavy burden not only for persons with disabilities but also for their families. It affects the range of choices that their families have in terms of the use of time, their social relationships and the management of economic, civil and political resources. The family dimension is likely to gain greater social and policy significance with the rapid ageing of the population and the related increase in the size of the population that experiences some degree of impairment.

Vulnerabilities in situations of conflict

232. Unprecedented waves of human displacement have followed in the wake of violent conflict and natural disasters. The latest estimates put the number of refugees at 12 million under the mandate of the Office of the United Nations High Commissioner for Refugees (UNHCR) and 4 million under the mandate of the United Nations Relief and Works Agency for Palestine Refugees in the Near East (UNWRA) in early 2001. The largest numbers of refugees are found in Asia (5 million) and Africa (4 million). The developed countries are host to 3 million refugees. It is believed that more that half of them are displaced owing to conflicts. While the number of refugees has decreased recently, the number of internally displaced persons who have been forced to flee their homes but have not reached a neighbouring country is on the rise. UNHCR estimates the current number of internally displaced

persons at 20 to 25 million in more than 40 countries. The rise in the number of internally displaced persons during the 1990s is a direct consequence of the increasing reluctance of many countries to host refugees. Approximately half of the world's refugees and internally displaced persons are children, while the other half is composed equally of men and women. However, predominantly male or female populations are found in specific situations involving refugees or internally displaced persons.

233. Internally displaced persons, particularly those who are neither protected nor attended to, are generally considered more vulnerable than other victims of conflict. However, some people who cannot afford to flee their homes may indeed be more vulnerable than internally displaced persons and refugees, as indicated by the examples of Angola and Afghanistan. In addition, displacement may result in improvements in internally displaced persons' lives, such as gaining access to health care and being able to attend school. They may also be able to decrease their vulnerability by becoming better informed and thus enhance their ability to identify risks and develop contingency plans.

234. Disempowerment of traditional community leaders, shifting gender and generational roles, and loss of access to common property have been identified as major sources of tension within displaced communities. In Africa and Asia, increased pressure on and competition for limited resources, employment and social services often generate tensions between displaced and host communities. However, when the presence of refugees or internally displaced persons is matched locally by significant foreign aid, the host community can often benefit from improved public services, such as health centres, schools and water points.

235. War provides a breeding ground for certain forms of gender-based violence, including exploitation, trafficking and mutilation, whether at home, in flight or in camps for displaced populations. Although men and boys do become victims of that kind of violence, women and girls are particularly vulnerable during conflict. Rape has been used systematically as a weapon of war. Although statistics may not do justice in accounting for the shocking reality of sexual violence, the figures are alarming. For instance, in Rwanda, as many as 250,000 to 500,000 women were

---

[61] "U.N. marks international day for rights awareness", *U.N. Wire*, 3 December 2002.

raped during the 1994 genocide.[62] Conflict also forces many women and girls to prostitute themselves in order to obtain basic commodities. The trauma for female victims of violence in particular continues even when the conflict is over, as they are shunned, ostracized and further stigmatized. They are also vulnerable to the increased domestic violence that tends to occur in the wake of armed violence.

236. Displacement further increases the vulnerability of women and girls to sexual violence and exploitation. For example, in Sierra Leone, 94 per cent of the displaced women and girls were victims of sexual violence.[63] Significant numbers of women and girls who have been separated from their families during conflict end up as sex workers, as they are left without support or livelihood. Many, bearing physical and emotional scars that will haunt them for life, lose hope of ever getting reintegrated into society and living normal lives.

237. During and after conflict situations women might assume new, untraditional roles, such as breadwinners or combatants. Women are also often forced by circumstances to display such behaviours as being assertive, wearing non-traditional dress or bearing a child of a man from the opposite party. Those behaviours may not be expected or accepted by their communities, making the women vulnerable to disapproval and sometimes punishment within those communities for stepping outside of the traditional boundaries.

238. During the past decade, it is estimated that 2 million children have been killed as a direct result of armed conflict; three times that many have been seriously injured or permanently disabled; and even greater numbers have died of malnutrition and disease. War conditions separate children from families and communities and deprive them of family care, health care, education, shelter and other essential services. The lack of education, in particular, has devastating effects on a population and on the development of a country as a whole.

239. Children face death, malnutrition, disease and violence, and sexual, physical and psychological abuse on an unprecedented scale in contemporary armed conflicts. In addition, children are often recruited by the warring parties to fight or provide services. Approximately 300,000 children under 18 years of age are currently serving as child soldiers in ongoing conflicts.[64] The United Nations Children's Fund (UNICEF) has suggested that as conflicts are prolonged, more and more children are recruited. Girls who have become child soldiers are often exploited sexually. The disruption of education eventually has a major detrimental impact on personal development and future prospects in life.

240. Inevitably, many of the children recruited into the military are deprived of their basic rights, including those related to family unity and education. Legal instruments for the protection of children, such as the Convention on the Rights of the Child and the Geneva Conventions are neither known nor respected in most inter-communal violent conflicts.

241. Older persons in situations of armed conflict are particularly susceptible to dislocation, disease, hunger and dehydration as compared with younger persons. Their relative lack of mobility can prevent them from leaving even if the water supply becomes contaminated, the land is littered with mines and supply sources are cut off. Older persons remain relatively invisible in post-conflict situations, partly because of the assumption by aid workers that they are being protected by families and neighbours but also because of triage: that is, the assignment of higher priority to younger generations, as they are considered more important for the family or community or more likely to survive from health-care interventions.

242. Research carried out by HelpAge International has revealed that older persons in conflict situations desire a restoration of conditions that will support their own self-sufficiency.[65] Further research under way by Global Action on Ageing is showing that in many places, older persons see themselves as being in charge

[62] Elisabeth Rehn and Ellen Johnson Sirleaf, *Women, War and Peace: The Independent Experts' Assessment on the Impact of Armed Conflict on Women and Women's Role in Peace-Building*, Progress of the World's Women, vol. 1 (New York, United Nations Development Fund for Women, 2002).

[63] Ibid.

[64] United Nations Children's Fund, *Adult Wars, Child Soldiers: Voices of Children Involved in Armed Conflict in the East Asia and Pacific Region* (New York, 2002).

[65] See, for example, HelpAge International and Office of the United Nations High Commissioner for Refugees, *Older People in Disasters and Humanitarian Crises: Guidelines for Best Practice* (London, HelpAge International, n.d.).

of the welfare of the family and that, being older, they feel that they have less to lose. They therefore take risks by attempting to intervene in beatings or kiliings, protect children or go out to collect provisions.

243. Older refugees make up from 11.5 to 30 per cent of refugee populations, and the majority are women. In addition to the problems experienced by older minorities, older refugees also commonly encounter social disintegration when support erodes and families become separated; negative social selection, when the weakest are left behind because a camp or centre empties out; and chronic dependency on an organization such as UNHCR for care and security.[66]

244. Violent conflicts cause physical and mental injuries, and many people face permanent disabilities. The use of mines, which often wound victims, creates large numbers of disabled persons. In particular, intra-State conflicts often target civilians, many of whom bear psychological scars that have to be addressed in peace-building efforts, and efforts have to be made to integrate them into society.

245. The needs of disabled persons, including rehabilitation at the community level and accessibility in terms of transport, housing, education and training, health services and employment have, so far, received limited attention in post-conflict peace-building programmes.

246. There are at present more humanitarian workers in conflict zones than ever before. However, aid workers are no longer as secure as they once were under the protection of the flag of the United Nations or the emblem of the International Red Cross or Red Crescent. Between August 1998 and December 2002, a total of 198 United Nations staff members were killed, and 240 were taken hostage or kidnapped. Hundreds more humanitarian workers have fallen victim to violent security incidents.

247. Threats against relief workers and peacekeeping personnel further restrict the ability of humanitarian organizations to ensure the delivery of assistance to vulnerable populations. In the Ituri region in the eastern part of the Democratic Republic of the Congo, following the brutal murder of six staff members of the International Committee of the Red Cross, humanitarian aid was reduced and staff withdrawn.

Restrictions on humanitarian access in Angola, Kosovo and Sierra Leone placed thousands at the mercy of the warring parties on whom they depended for basic supplies. Journalists have also been direct targets in conflict. Close to 500 journalists have been killed worldwide since 1990, many of them silenced to prevent accurate reporting of atrocities.

248. Clearly, conflict situations and displacement uproot people from their familiar environment, traditional support and protection networks (family and community) and existing authority structure (such as traditional community leaders). They also deprive people of resources that normally would have been available to them. As a result, persons in situations of conflict are exposed to greater risks and often face increased social vulnerability. Moreover, displacement exposes populations to risks specific to refugee status inside and outside the country of origin, such as abuse, violation of rights and exclusion from access to social services.

Traditional knowledge and cultures of indigenous peoples

249. For indigenous peoples, the preservation of their culture is essential for their survival, existence and development. It encompasses their languages, knowledge, traditions, histories, customs, arts, crafts and music. Maintaining and revitalizing cultural expression is becoming a vital component of many indigenous development strategies. Unfortunately, indigenous peoples face pressure from many forces that undermine their culture, such as conflict with non-indigenous values and discrimination. That pressure, together with the forces that cause indigenous peoples to be dislocated from ancestral lands, threaten the core of indigenous identity and survival.

250. Globalization and the attendant homogenization of societies worldwide, by and large according to Western values, are major factors undermining indigenous cultures. Faster transportation and communication shatter the isolation of many indigenous peoples, exposing them to modern ideas and ways of life. Within indigenous communities, younger generations who are adapting to modern ways and migrating to urban areas are reluctant to hold onto traditional knowledge. Their reluctance is reinforced by the external bias against traditional knowledge. Furthermore, since traditional knowledge is transmitted

---

[66] United Nations, "No safety net for older migrants and refugees" (DPI/2264).

orally, there is a risk that it will be lost with the last remaining generation of indigenous peoples.

251. In Latin America, for example, some indigenous communities have, since pre-Hispanic times, attained and maintained sustainability in the administration of justice, health and healing, and in the educational system. However, a fact-finding mission by the World Intellectual Property Organization (WIPO) found that modern cultural influences and pressures are rapidly changing indigenous ways of life and endangering the survival of their traditions, culture and knowledge.[67]

252. Culture is jeopardized when its expressions such as folklore, art, crafts and music are exploited, commercialized and subsequently copyrighted or patented under the Western system of intellectual property rights. That legal framework typically fails to protect the traditional knowledge and cultural heritage of indigenous peoples, who emphasize collective ownership of all their resources. The situation is further exacerbated by the willingness and openness of indigenous peoples to share their knowledge and culture, consistent with their philosophy on communal rights and their oral tradition. The wanton transfer of traditions, cultures and their symbols to the modern world without their being fully understood also leads to incorrect interpretations that ultimately debase those elements that indigenous peoples consider sacred. Although increasing indigenous activism and public awareness have recently, in some cases of patent recognition, led to decisions in favour of indigenous communities, the battle on that front continues.

253. Another factor that leads to the undermining of indigenous culture is the discriminatory or racist treatment of indigenous peoples, including discrimination in the justice system.[68] A deliberate policy of abolishing indigenous culture through assimilation is historically an approach by which modern society seeks to minimize conflicts with indigenous peoples. Such discriminatory policy is based on the perception that indigenous culture is undesirable or inferior and incompatible with modern

society and economy. For example, WIPO found that indigenous culture and cosmology were systematically misinterpreted and misrepresented, resulting in the further negative stereotyping of indigenous peoples.[69] It is interesting to note that while indigenous peoples are negatively stereotyped for their medicinal practices, corporations have been active in bioprospecting for new medicines based on the knowledge of indigenous peoples about the medicinal value of plants.

254. Multinational pharmaceutical corporations have been aggressive in exploring and gaining control of traditional indigenous medicines and in registering sacred plants as if they had been developed in a laboratory. Examples include the now-revoked patents on neem and turmeric, two medicinal plants used in India from time immemorial based on traditional knowledge.[70] The patent on ayahuasca (or yage), a plant considered sacred by the indigenous peoples of Amazonia, is now under litigation. A patent on quinoa was granted based on the supposed invention by researchers, but the quinoa plant has long been a food staple for the indigenous peoples in Bolivia's Altiplano. If the patent came into force, there was a risk that it would impair the indigenous communities' capacity to sell their own agricultural products, and that improved varieties might eventually be imported into Bolivia at higher prices.[71]

255. Globalization, homogenization and westernization of societies as well as the folkorization of tradition are among the many forces that tend to undermine indigenous cultures and weaken the ability of indigenous peoples to sustain their traditional livelihoods. Against that background, and faced with routine discrimination, the very survival of many indigenous communities has been and continues to be at stake.

Conclusion

256. Various forms of sociocultural biases and formal and informal discrimination lead to social exclusion resulting in social vulnerability among individuals,

67 World Intellectual Property Organization, *Intellectual Property Needs and Expectations of Traditional Knowledge Holders: WIPO Report on Fact-Finding Missions on Intellectual Property and Traditional Knowledge (1998-1999)* (Geneva, 2001).
68 Australian Royal Commission into Aboriginal Deaths in Custody, Australian Aboriginal deaths in custody reports.

69 WIPO, *Intellectual Property Needs and Expectations of Traditional Knowledge Holders*.
70 Chakravarthi Raghavan, "Neem patent revoked by European Patent Office", *Third World Network*, 11 May 2000.
71 WIPO, *Intellectual Property Needs and Expectations of Traditional Knowledge Holders*.

households and disadvantaged groups and communities. Stereotyping of any kind hinders the cause of social integration by fostering misperceptions, bias and discrimination. Persons with disabilities, women, migrants, indigenous peoples and older persons all face misperceptions in their struggles for social acceptance and integration. Certain existing institutions, social structures and practices, including such generally accepted ones as professional licensing and other formal requirements also constitute de facto

barriers preventing the full participation by all members of society. Therefore, the task for social policy makers is not limited to ridding societies of prejudice, misperception and open discrimination. What is required is a closer and more comprehensive examination of social institutions, structures and accepted practices, with a view to making necessary changes in order to correct any unintended effects they might have on social integration.

Part two
Policy challenges

Introduction

257. As noted earlier, the terms "vulnerability" and "vulnerable" are often loosely used in policy formulation and have not been subjected to much theoretical rigour or analytical scrutiny. While the analytical use of the concept of vulnerability is largely concerned with situation-specific (risk-specific) vulnerabilities, policy references to vulnerability mainly relate to the attributes of social groups. Thus, children, women, older persons, persons with disabilities, indigenous people and migrants are usually considered as particularly vulnerable in view of their high level of social and economic dependency and exposure to specific social risks.

258. Vulnerability initially emerged as a benchmark for social policy interventions in a context in which poverty eradication had become the overarching principle guiding social development interventions. Further, in developing countries, vulnerability has provided the measure and the moral ground for a multitude of community-scale social projects targeting poor and disadvantaged groups through such instruments as social funds.

259. Part two of the report consists of four chapters. Chapter IV deals with vulnerabilities related to employment. A large body of evidence suggests that that form of vulnerability is, across the board, the major claim on society in both developed and developing countries. Three levels of employment-related vulnerabilities are delineated. First, and to a significant extent, concerns with employment reflect a basic economic reality: the persistence of situations of high unemployment in many developed countries; and underemployment and a dearth of decent jobs in most of the developing world. Secondly, the scope of people's worries about employment goes beyond the critical and pervasive issue of the lack of employment opportunities. Large demographic segments, such as women, young people and older persons and several social groups, including persons with disabilities and indigenous people, have been calling for policies to remove the physical, institutional, cultural and legal obstacles that limit their access to employment. Finally, employment-related vulnerabilities rest on a major policy failure: employment issues have continued to remain peripheral to the overall development policy agenda despite the centrality of employment in the fight against poverty and social exclusion.

260. Chapter V highlights the importance of shifting policy emphasis towards social integration, putting it at the centre of social development, as well as the concomitant need for social protection. What is to be gained by promoting the social integration of groups in society — the value proposition — and the importance of doing so are best illustrated by the policy frameworks that are being independently developed in reference to the advancement of persons with disabilities, older persons and indigenous peoples. The chapter focuses on the need for and the challenges of developing approaches that account for both social protection and social inclusion. In particular, in the wake of the recent economic crises that affected several countries in East Asia and Latin America, the issue of social protection is being visited anew. The fact that large numbers of middle-class workers suddenly found themselves and their families extremely vulnerable to income loss has dramatically

exposed the insufficiencies of existing social protection frameworks as well as the limits of traditional family and community-based support systems. Discussions on such issues as urbanization, family changes and ageing, which until now had been largely held from a long-term perspective, have been given a sense of urgency, with suggestions coming from all quarters that a new approach to the management of social risks is needed.

261. Chapter VI focuses on a rights-based approach to social and developmental issues, which has gained importance over the past decade. According to this line of thinking, social vulnerabilities are viewed mainly as the outcome of a rights deficit. Therefore, ascertaining and promoting the rights of the various social groups is key to their empowerment. Three attempts to develop a rights-based approach are reviewed in relation to the advancement of indigenous people, migrants and persons with a disability.

262. Finally, chapter VII deals with the role of international cooperation in reducing vulnerabilities. So far, reduction of vulnerability from an international assistance perspective has been primarily considered within the context of humanitarian emergencies. However, reconsideration of poverty issues in the light of recent economic and social development points to the relevance of a vulnerability reduction approach as part of international cooperation for social development.

IV. Addressing barriers to employment

263. Providing access to decent, safe and productive work to the very large number of the world's unemployed, underemployed and working poor is and remains one of the most daunting policy challenges. Recent estimates by the International Labour Organization put the number of unemployed worldwide at 180 million at the end of 2002 — an increase of 20 million since 2001 — and the number of working poor (workers living on one dollar or less a day) at 550 million. Against that bleak background, it is anticipated that about 400 million young people will be joining the world labour force by the end of 2010, of whom 60 per cent are in Asia and 15 per cent in sub-Saharan Africa. If the Millennium Development Goal of halving the proportion of people whose income is less than one dollar a day by 2015 is to be achieved, the number of jobs that will need to be created by the end of the present decade is on the order of one billion. Furthermore, protracted conditions of high unemployment and/or pervasive underemployment tend to undermine the social fabric of societies and challenge the very concept of social development.

264. Employment lies at the core of individuals' perception and experience of income security versus economic vulnerability; social participation versus social exclusion; human dignity versus exploitation. The centrality of employment in the fight against poverty and social exclusion was a central message of the World Summit for Social Development.

265. Nevertheless, macroeconomic policies, as exemplified by the Washington Consensus, emphasize the role of the market, inflation control and the minimal role of the State. In that policy scenario, full employment is not set as a primary macroeconomic objective, and employment outcomes are largely left to market forces. It is in this sense that employment issues have remained largely as an afterthought on the overall development agenda.

266. Particularly worrying is the fact that developing countries have not been successful in generating productive employment, not even some of the countries that have experienced strong economic growth. Employment creation in modern sectors has fallen short of compensating for the labour released by declining industries and has failed to absorb the large cohorts of new entrants into the labour force. As a result, many workers formerly employed in the formal sector have resorted to informal activities, and access to productive employment by young people has been significantly reduced. In 2000, approximately half of total employment in Latin America and about three fourths of total employment in other developing regions was generated in the informal economy.

267. The slow growth of employment in the formal sector and the related expansion of the informal economy have resulted in unstable and often declining earnings, growing inequality in wages and social protection coverage between skilled and unskilled workers and between younger and older workers, and higher levels of working poor. A number of surveys have suggested that under such circumstances certain segments of the population, particularly the young, have developed feelings of economic vulnerability and fatalistic views of life as well as a loss of trust in the market economy, the value of education and even sometimes in democracy.

268. How the employment crisis is addressed will influence the future course of all economies, whether developed or developing, given their interdependence in a globalizing world. It is critical to make employment creation central to all economic and social policies. To do so requires an integrated approach to those policies. Two initiatives, the Global Employment Agenda and the Youth Employment Network, have recently been undertaken with the firm resolve to place employment creation at the centre of economic and social policies, nationally and globally.

269. The Global Employment Agenda, an initiative of the International Labour Organization, signals a significant change in policy approach. It intends to elaborate a comprehensive employment framework that will allow for policy coherence and coordination. That objective is based on the premise that, as a condition of success, it is vital to address employment generation explicitly rather than relying on the trickle-down effect of macroeconomic policies, as is currently the case. In the Millennium Declaration (resolution 55/2 of 8 September 2000), the General Assembly resolved to develop and implement strategies that give young people everywhere a real chance to find decent and productive work. The Youth Employment Network,

an initiative of the Secretary-General,[72] aims at providing the momentum and general policy framework for translating that commitment into action.

270. It appears that the current high unemployment and wage inequality observed in many developed countries are the result of the slow pace at which demand, output and investment have been expanding over the past two decades. The answer lies in appropriate macroeconomic policies to increase productive investment and expand employment. Under such conditions, trade and technology can reinforce economic growth, job creation and productivity gains. It is only with such an approach, reducing unemployment by demand management and high growth rates, that the vulnerabilities of employment can be addressed directly in order to promote labour market security as the norm for working people.

271. Rapid and sustained growth in major industrial economies, combined with the provision of greater market access for the exports of developing countries, would enable developing countries to better address their development challenges and labour-market problems. In order to improve labour-market conditions in the present policy environment, it will be necessary to rethink development policies at the national and global levels. In particular, serious consideration needs to be given to the speed and pattern of integration of developing countries into the global economy. Rapid and premature liberalization, compounded by ineffective or misguided policy reforms and applied in the absence of appropriate institutions and productive capacity, has led to worsened labour market conditions in a number of developing countries. The crisis in Asia demonstrated that volatile capital flows and economic policy errors can upset the economic momentum of even the strongest developing countries, with serious consequences for wages, employment and social conditions.

272. Addressing the employment vulnerability of young people requires a two-pronged approach. One is to improve their employability by enhancing their job skills so they become more attractive to employers and are thus better able to compete in the job market. A second is to remove barriers, whether they be legislative or perceptive, which can lead to discriminatory employment practices against youth.

---

[72] See General Assembly resolution 56/117 of 19 December 2001.

273. Faced with the limited success of youth measures, as explained in chapter I of the present report, much hope has been put in a new approach that will be promoted within the framework of the Youth Employment Network: removing barriers leading to practices that discriminate against youth employment in general, the employment of young women or youth entrepreneurship. The Youth Employment Network places great value on the involvement of young people as partners in policy formulation and development. It also emphasizes the contribution of employment policies to social cohesion and inclusion, echoing similar claims made by other social groups, such as older persons or persons with disabilities.

274. Older persons wishing to begin their own small businesses often confront difficulties similar to those encountered by youth in gaining access to credit. In some cases, explicit age barriers prevent older persons from qualifying for microcredit schemes or low-interest loans. Changes in credit policy can help older persons who are motivated to do so become entrepreneurs, making use of the experience and skills they have gained over their lifetime to build successful microenterprises.

275. Enacting effective employment policies for older persons requires a flexible approach. Those older persons who are willing and able to work should have the opportunity to do so and should avail themselves of flexible working conditions. Programmes to retrain them and upgrade their skills should be available so that they can keep pace with technological and other changes in the workplace.

276. As stated previously, in developing countries, opportunities for the integration of persons with disabilities through employment largely rest on self-employment. Lessons from existing pilot projects indicate the critical importance of identifying productive activities for which there is a potential demand and with low start-up costs but which involve tasks that are within the reach of persons with disabilities. The provision of training on all aspects of small business operations is also critical, including production, processing, marketing and business management. In order for those initiatives to work, however, local banks and other lending institutions have to be encouraged to include persons with disabilities in their credit schemes, which involves breaking down stereotypes about the creditworthiness and potential productivity of those individuals.

Recommendations

277. Experiences in the last two decades of the twentieth century clearly show that a reorientation of macroeconomic policy to explicitly target employment creation is needed in both industrialized and developing countries in order to reduce poverty and vulnerability in a permanent fashion. The shift in policy focus would be a concrete, practical example of the integration of social and economic policies; it is an approach that is widely embraced. The implementation of employment creation policy is complex: it must meet the challenges presented by various economic sectors and attend to the concerns of diverse social groups, as well as address gender-based discrimination.

278. The appropriate macroeconomic policies are those that result in an increase in productive investment and employment-intensive growth, and they should be advanced. Trade and diffusion of technology can reinforce economic growth, job creation and productivity gains when macroeconomic policy that promotes job-creating growth is in place.

279. Industrialized economies should be encouraged to provide greater market access for the goods exported from developing countries as a means of supporting development and improving existing labour-market conditions in those countries through export growth. A number of international agreements (including World Trade Organization agreements) call for the phasing out of all forms of export subsidies, for substantial reductions in trade-distorting domestic support and for the improvement of market access for the developing countries. In that context, market access for exports of developing countries is not a matter of charity.

280. Development policies should be refashioned so as to guard against premature liberalization and misguided policy reforms that, in the absence of appropriate institutions and productive capacity, can worsen labour-market conditions in developing countries.

281. The youth unemployment problem should be addressed through a combination of efforts to improve young people's employability by enhancing their job skills and by removing legislative and other barriers that can lead to discriminatory practices adversely affecting youth employment.

282. Credit policies should be modified so as to enable older persons, women and young people who wish to start their own businesses to have greater access to microcredit and other loan schemes.

283. Older persons should have the opportunity to continue working and contributing to the economy for as long as they wish. To that end, older men and women should be able to avail themselves of retraining and skills-upgrading programmes to help them keep up with technological and other work-based changes.

284. Persons with disabilities in developing countries should be supported in their efforts to better integrate into the mainstream economy through wider participation in the labour market. Opportunities for self-employment should be encouraged, including improved access to credit schemes, along with the provision of training on all aspects of small business operations.

285. In developed countries, it is important to mainstream disabled men and women into open employment rather than direct them into sheltered or supported work environments.

V. Promoting social integration and social protection

286. Of all social groups, persons with disabilities, indigenous peoples and, more recently, older persons have been the most active in articulating a vision that puts social integration at the centre of social development. The claims made by the groups rest on the understanding that the success of social policy revolves around a proper balance between empowerment, social inclusion and social protection. It is a vision that also suggests that building inclusive and cohesive societies should be at the top of the policy agenda.

287. Social protection is an important component of an integrated approach to reducing social vulnerability, complementing policy measures aimed at preventing social exclusion. However, recent experience with targeted social protection measures and the implementation of Poverty Reduction Strategy Papers in developing countries has highlighted the need to pursue a comprehensive strategy. It calls for a careful comparison of the long-term total social costs and benefits of various measures and a respect for differences between countries, rather than a "one size fits all" approach.

Equalization of opportunities for persons with disabilities

288. The term "disability" encompasses a great number of different functional limitations. People may have physical, intellectual or sensory impairments, medical conditions or mental illness. Such impairments, conditions or illnesses may be permanent or transitory in nature. Persons with a disability are not inherently vulnerable. However, as a result of environmental factors, a disability can become a handicap. The term "handicap" means the loss or limitation of opportunities to take part in the life of the community on an equal level with others. It describes the encounter between the person with a disability and the environment. The purpose of the term is to emphasize the focus on the shortcomings in the environment and in many organized activities in society, such as, information, communication and education, that prevent persons with disabilities from participating on equal terms with the non-disabled.

289. Current definitions of a person with a disability such the *International Classification of Functioning, Disability and Health (ICF)*, adopted by the World Health Organization in 2001, stress that a person's functioning or disability lies in a dynamic interaction between health conditions and environmental and personal factors. This approach to disability represents a fundamental shift from a focus on physical, sensory or developmental abilities to a focus on opportunities in society and on the centrality of social inclusion. The key issue is access by individuals to choice in decisions about their well-being, livelihoods and civil and political participation, without recourse to aid or assistance. In this sense, economic self-sufficiency is not viewed in terms of an individual's ability to earn income but in terms of the individual's capacity to influence and control economic resources as well as to address risk and uncertainty.

290. The ability of people with disabilities to make social and economic contributions and achieve sustainable livelihoods is determined by the extent to which they are able to overcome individual, social and environmental barriers that restrict access to social and economic opportunities. They must also be enabled to pass through the following stages of physical and social integration: (a) adapting to a disabling condition and maximizing functional capacity; (b) interacting with the community and with society; and (c) gaining access to types of social and economic activities that give life meaning and purpose, which include contributing to one's family and community, actively participating in society or obtaining productive and gainful employment.

291. From the disability perspective, policy guidance for the design of positive measures to address social vulnerability is provided by the Standard Rules on the Equalization of Opportunities for Persons with Disabilities, in particular Rules 5 through 8. Rule 5 addresses accessibility to the physical environment and to information and communication. In the design of policy options to address social vulnerability, universal design concepts and principles provide a basis to assess accessibility with reference to interactions between people and the wider environment. The value proposition of universal design is that the design of products and environments should be usable by all people to the greatest extent possible. The same

universal principle underpins Rules 6 through 8, which deal with measures to ensure equal opportunities to participate in mainstream education; exercise the basic right to seek productive and gainful employment in open labour markets; and have access to appropriate social safety nets in terms of income maintenance and services.

292. For purposes of policy design and evaluation, it is important to distinguish between access and accessibility. Access is not an act or a state but rather refers to freedom of choice in entering, approaching, communicating with or making use of a situation.[73] Equal participation occurs if equalization of opportunities to participate is provided through measures that enhance accessibility.

293. Policy concern with environmental accessibility reflects a shift in emphasis from medical models of disability, with their emphasis on care, protection and assistance to persons with disabilities in adapting to "normal" social structures, to social models with a focus on empowerment, participation and modifications of environments to promote equalization of opportunities for all.[74]

294. Fostering sustainable livelihoods for people with disabilities involves addressing all types of barriers simultaneously in ways that facilitate the passage of people with disabilities through the various stages of physical and social integration. It would require local, national and international disability strategies based upon comprehensive and integrated combinations, including (a) rehabilitation strategies that maximize the functional capabilities of people with disabilities; (b) inclusion and empowerment strategies to facilitate their active participation in their communities, societies and economies; and (c) architectural and design strategies that remove and prevent unnecessary barriers in infrastructure, including transportation systems, technology and communications, and other features of the physical environment.

295. Some persons may have disabilities so severe that they cannot pass successfully through all three stages of physical and social integration and are therefore at risk, or vulnerable. Members of this subgroup would therefore require services both to augment asset capacities and to reduce the potential of risk. Those needs can be addressed through the provision of specialized support services throughout the person's life (for instance, ongoing personal assistance services). However, all such services must be developed as part of comprehensive inclusion and empowerment strategies that promote sustainable livelihoods, social integration and the well-being of persons with disabilities.

296. To address vulnerability and the advancement of persons with disabilities, it is necessary to recognize that persons with a disability do not represent a homogeneous group. Moreover, persons with a disability, for policy purposes, are defined by a condition rather than by an attribute, as in the case of international instruments concerned with gender or the rights of children (a cohort-determined group).

297. It is best to approach an analysis of policy and programme responses to vulnerability in terms of action to prevent or reduce conditions in the environment that affect the mobilization of assets or the creation of opportunities to participate on the basis of equality in social life and development. Such action is a theme of the proposed comprehensive and integral international convention to promote and protect the rights and dignity of persons with disabilities, which was endorsed by the General Assembly in its resolution 56/168 of 19 December 2001.[75]

298. The aim of the convention is for all citizens to be involved as agents and beneficiaries of global development; none should be excluded from the process.[76] A major issue in the elaboration of a convention is the identification of strategic options to bring the disability perspective into mainstream international development instruments, such as the Millennium Development Goals which do not specifically address the situation of persons with disabilities.

---

[73] Scott Campbell Brown, "Methodological paradigms that shape disability research", in *Handbook of Disability Studies*, Gary L. Albrecht, Katherine D. Seelman and Michael Bury, editors (Thousand Oaks, California, Sage Publications, 2001).

[74] Office of the Deputy President, "Situation analysis", in *Integrated National Disability Strategy: White Paper*, chap. 1 (Government of South Africa, 1997).

[75] Available from http://www.un.org/esa/socdev/enable/disA56168e1.htm

[76] Statement by the President of Mexico, Vicente Fox, at the fifty-sixth session of the General Assembly, 10 November 2001.

Indigenous identities and aspirations

299. Marginalization and discriminatory practices have historically been the primary sources of vulnerability of indigenous peoples and eventually led to their struggle for recognition, equality, self-determination and the right to development according to their own values and culture. The ultimate goal of indigenous peoples is to be recognized as distinct cultures, valued as peoples and given the economic, social and cultural opportunities to ensure their basic right to self-determination and cultural survival.

300. Indigenous peoples from different walks of life have organized and led the dialogue between their own societies and the dominant culture. The paradigm has shifted from an assimilation model and welfare-based interaction with mainstream societies to one that is more open to the articulated demands and aspirations of indigenous peoples. The replacement of ILO Convention No. 107 concerning the Protection and Integration of Indigenous and Other Tribal and Semi-Tribal Populations in Independent Countries, which promoted the assimilation of indigenous populations with a view to protecting their health and welfare, by ILO Convention No. 169 concerning Indigenous and Tribal Peoples in Independent Countries, which recognizes the identity of indigenous peoples and their rights to participate in decision-making regarding their own destiny emphasizes the shift in conceptual approach.

301. Bound by a common struggle for their rights, indigenous peoples bring a diverse set of issues to the negotiating table. Some are concerned primarily with land, others with culture. Some indigenous peoples push to preserve their way of life; while others subscribe to full participation in the material and cultural life of the societies around them while simultaneously maintaining their own identities. In any case, the fundamental principle on which the advancement and empowerment of indigenous people is to be based is the recognition that indigenous traditions and ways of life, while being valuable in their own right, also contribute extensive and useful knowledge of medicinal plants, sustainable agriculture and approaches to environmental and ecological protection and conservation to the entire world community.

302. The resolution of indigenous land claims and cultural rights ultimately rests within States. Political and judicial systems as well as social and cultural justice in each State are central to policies granting of indigenous rights. Development objectives of both the State and the indigenous peoples need to be weighed, reconciling points of conflict. Pressure from the international community lends support to the struggle of indigenous peoples.

303. In this context, it is critical to formulate and enact laws that secure the rights of indigenous peoples and protect them from institutional racism and discrimination. The international human rights instruments should provide the standards for an effective framework in that respect. In addition, it is essential for indigenous peoples to participate fully in the design, implementation and evaluation of policies and programmes addressing their problems.

304. It is very important to encourage and support the dialogue between indigenous peoples and mainstream society, particularly through forums within the United Nations and other international organizations. Such forums provide a vehicle to sustain awareness of the plight of indigenous peoples and to allow them to present their case to States, the international media and civil society at large. The forums are an essential component of the process that will ensure that all stakeholders in modern and indigenous societies can arrive at solutions to problems in a peaceful and effective manner.

A society for all ages

305. For the majority of older persons, situations of risk and vulnerability increase with age. Older persons possess both strengths and vulnerabilities accumulated since childhood that have an impact on their ability to manage risk and insecurity in later life. As one advances in age, transitions are typically intensified, and the likelihood of stressful life events increases.

306. Older persons are not by definition vulnerable, but as a group they share some common basic features that are considered to generate a set of shared problems, particularly with advancing age. Although ageing is not a risk in itself, as persons reach the higher ages, they are often forced to adjust themselves to situations over which they may have little control, and their physical, social, psychological and economic circumstances in life will determine their ability to respond to situations of adversity, be they chronic

diseases, loss of physical strength and material well-being, widowhood, discrimination, conflict or emergencies. Hence, tension develops between vulnerability and independence — when an independent past is at odds with an emerging need for care and reliance on others. Older persons' responses will depend on the suitability of their own defences built up over a lifetime, the presence and level of outside sources of support and their ability to adapt to new situations that arise as a result of the risk.

307. The main factors that make older persons vulnerable in society — exclusion, discrimination, lack of social protection — are overlapping and cross-sectoral issues that go far beyond ageing and are part and parcel of development and human rights. That view was recognized at the Second World Assembly on Ageing in 2002, which called for ageing to be mainstreamed into all policy areas, with particular emphasis on national development frameworks and poverty eradication strategies. The Madrid International Plan of Action on Ageing acknowledged the significant advances over the past decade that went beyond the narrow social welfare concerns and linked ageing to development, giving legitimacy to efforts to address ageing within a framework of poverty reduction, participation, gender equality and human rights. Thus, in order to move on to the next level, the Madrid Plan of Action has called for ageing to be linked to development issues and embedded into development targets and agendas.

308. For the most part, however, both development institutions and national Governments have largely ignored the impact of a growing older population in their development strategies. References to older generations are dramatically absent from International Development Targets and the Millennium Development Goals. Yet the backdrop for the targets and discussions is demographic ageing, a phenomenon that is gathering enough force to make obsolete many policy recommendations on poverty eradication, health and employment that do not take into consideration either the large numbers of persons entering old age who will be able to contribute to the development processes on those who will require social protection and care. Addressing the reasons for the exclusion of millions from the overall development process and from development targets and poverty eradication strategies in particular should be a major concern of policy makers.

309. The challenges posed by population ageing are enormous, not only for older persons and their families, but also for the community and society at large. Consequently, policies that reduce the vulnerability of older persons also result in gains for the family, society and future generations — a potentially win-win situation.

Limitations of and difficulties with targeted approaches

310. During the 1990s, the priority given to poverty eradication and good governance triggered a shift in the approach to social protection, from a universal benefits perspective towards highly targeted transfers. The main argument in favour of the move to targeted transfer programmes is that, in lower and middle income countries, universal social programmes have proven inefficient, costly and unsustainable; that they are biased towards the middle class; and that they do not benefit the poor and the most vulnerable. While there still is a consensus on the need to target the scarce public resources that are available for social protection, the debate on targeted versus universal approaches has been reopened in the wake of the recent financial crises in Asia and Latin America.

311. The fact that a wide spectrum of people affected by those economic crises, both poor and non-poor, suddenly appeared vulnerable, without any means of support, and that many children had to leave school out of economic necessity prompted the realization that some form of universal social protection was needed to mitigate the social consequences of such crises. That view has been reinforced by the further realization that in a globalizing world no developing country, however economically successful, is immune from volatility driven by fluctuations in international trade and capital flows.

312. Obviously, safety nets that focus only on the poor fall short of providing a framework for broad-based emergency intervention. An assessment of the various social safety net responses implemented after the crises finds that success was most likely under the following circumstances: when the responses built on pre-existing, well-functioning programmes; when the institutional and delivery capacity of central and local agencies was sufficient to cope with rapid expansion; when budgetary allocations were adequate; and when redistributive and poverty alleviation efforts were

driven by political will and commitment, a dimension often missing when safety nets are entirely supported from external funds.

313. However, more fundamental questions have been raised as to the difficulty of targeting adequately and assuring its social sustainability in non-emergency contexts. One of the strongest arguments in favour of targeting is that it is cost-effective, as it aims to get benefits into the hands of those who need them most, with minimal distribution to the non-needy. However, from a social inclusion and empowerment standpoint, the economic benefits of the approach may be offset by its social costs. In addition to the feelings of stigmatization that targeting can generate, there is a danger that the non-targeted group will grow resentful of those receiving assistance. In some cases, there may be little that separates a target group from a non-target group in terms of need. Moreover, targeting often involves high administrative costs, reducing the resources going to the selected groups.

314. Under a targeted system, the determination of who receives assistance versus who does not can be based on a variety of factors external to the individual or group level of need, such as donor preferences, programme design, political considerations or geographical location. One of the more promising forms involves community-based targeting, where the community is directly involved in identifying beneficiaries, using eligibility criteria of their own choosing. Not only are people at the community level more likely than programme administrators to be aware of the actual circumstances in which people live, the participatory process itself can be quite empowering for the community, as it increases local control over programmes. Thus, community-based targeting is attractive on two main fronts: one, it draws upon local knowledge, thereby increasing accuracy; and two, it involves beneficiaries directly in the decision-making process, thereby promoting equity and inclusion.

315. Community-based targeting may, however, have some disadvantages as well. Decision makers in the community may divert assistance away from the neediest to their own families and friends. Another danger is that the process can become highly divisive, causing resentment and tension in the community between those chosen for assistance and those left out. Experience with community-based targeting suggests that its success is highly contingent on local sociocultural contexts and eventually rests on the

development of a politically sustainable social contract. That lesson may be of general value to any small or large-scale effort to develop some permanent form of social assistance.

Poverty Reduction Strategy Papers and social protection

316. Recognition of the multidimensional nature of poverty lies at the core of the principles underlying the development of Poverty Reduction Strategy Papers (PRSPs). About two thirds of the Papers explicitly discuss social protection issues, although the depth to which they are addressed, and the extent to which policies intended to promote social protection are elaborated vary considerably.[77] That reflects a belief that social protection plays a limited and optional role rather than an integral one in poverty reduction.

317. Overall, the social protection measures mentioned in the PRSPs also appear to be weakly redistributive. Where redistribution occurs, it is mainly through increased expenditures on public services for the poorest. Thus, in the PRSPs, social protection has primarily been dealt with in terms of its ability to alleviate the worst effects of poverty rather than in terms of its potential to help people escape from poverty.

318. A striking feature of the PRSPs is that none of the strategies make the connection between social protection and measures to ensure that poor people benefit from economic growth, implying that social protection is not seen as one of the tools for redistribution and development. Furthermore, one finds little sense of coordination among policies to promote the social inclusion of the poorest and most marginalized groups on the one hand, and development on the other hand. This oversight is all the more puzzling as several papers have been elaborated in countries where there is evidence of decline in "traditional" social safety nets as a result of the breakdown of the extended family system, urbanization, rural migration or economic hardships.

319. Evaluation of the impact of social protection measures, to the extent they existed in the PRSPs,

---

[77] Rachel Marcus and John Wilkinson, "Whose poverty matters? Vulnerability, social protection and PRSPs", Working Paper No. 1 (London, Childhood Poverty Research and Policy Centre [CHIP], 2002).

suggests that coverage was low and largely inadequate.[78] Measures tended to concentrate on livelihood, income support and access to key services. Cash transfers were an important element of some interim PRSPs, particularly those of countries with economies in transition. Nevertheless, as a result of resource restrictions, cash allowances were reportedly so low that few people actually availed themselves of the assistance. Pensions were mentioned in about one third of the PRSPs, focusing primarily on old-age pensions, although disability and war veteran pensions were mentioned to a limited degree. Once again, however, owing to resource limitations, coverage was low and inadequate.

320. A number of countries continue to rely fully on user fees for such fundamental social services as primary education and preventive health care, a practice that excludes the neediest and runs counter to the poverty-reduction goals of the PRSPs. Therefore, the benefits of facilitating people's access to basic services, such as health care and clean water, by waiving user fees or providing scholarships so that poor children can attend school should be promoted more systematically within the framework of the PRSPs.

321. Revisiting the PRSP process in the context of the Millennium Development Goals and other commitments made at earlier United Nations conferences and summits and their follow-up processes is encouraging, necessary and logical. It provides an opportunity to extend the formulation and implementation of the PRSPs beyond their present scope, particularly in focusing on comprehensive measures that have tangible benefits for poor people.

Recommendations

322. Discrimination and social or cultural biases will not automatically disappear with a reduction in poverty. Explicit policy measures and strict enforcement of legal protection are needed to address and rectify barriers to social integration.

323. Barriers to social equity and social integration deprive marginalized populations not only of the ability to protect their economic rights and achieve their full potential in contributing to society, but also of the opportunity to earn adequate income. Therefore, policy measures to reduce social vulnerability need to be based on an integrated approach to the problem, keeping in mind the appropriate priorities to maximize the effectiveness of such policy responses.

324. A society for all — girls and boys, men and women — encompasses the goal of providing all social groups with the opportunity to contribute to society. To work towards that goal, it is necessary to remove whatever excludes or discriminates against them and to enable their full participation in decision-making

325. With a view towards fostering sustainable livelihoods for people with disabilities, national and international efforts should promote rehabilitation strategies that maximize the functional capacities of persons with disabilities; architectural and design strategies that remove unnecessary barriers in the environment; and inclusion and empowerment strategies that facilitate greater participation in society.

326. Persons with disabilities should be granted equal opportunities to participate in mainstream education, to seek productive and gainful employment in open labour markets and to have access to appropriate social safety nets in terms of income maintenance and services.

327. As proposed in the Standard Rules on the Equalization of Opportunities for Persons with Disabilities, universal design concepts should be advanced to ensure that products and environments are usable by all people to the greatest extent possible. Improving accessibility of persons with disabilities to the physical environment and to information and communication technologies will help them overcome barriers that restrict their access to social and economic opportunities.

328. Using the international human rights instruments as a framework, laws and policies should be formulated and enacted to protect the rights of indigenous peoples and guard them against institutional racism and discrimination. Issues concerning land rights and the protection of indigenous peoples' cultures warrant particular consideration. The full participation of indigenous peoples in the design, implementation and evaluation of those laws and policies should be guaranteed as part of an open dialogue between indigenous peoples and mainstream society.

---

[78] Ibid.

329. Although as a group older persons are not inherently vulnerable, the ageing process can force people to adjust to physical, social and economic circumstances over which they have little control, increasing their level of risk. Older persons' vulnerabilities can be significantly reduced through a combination of their own defences built up over a lifetime and the presence of outside sources of support.

330. Policy makers, including development institutions and national Governments, should pay greater attention to the impact of a growing older population on their development strategies, being mindful of the contributions that older men and women can make to the development process as well as the demands they will place on social protection and care services.

331. As recognized at the Second World Assembly on Ageing in 2002, ageing should be mainstreamed into all policy areas, most notably into national development frameworks and poverty reduction strategies. Furthermore, issues concerning older persons should be addressed within a context of poverty reduction, participation, gender equality and human rights, and linked to development targets and agendas.

332. Given the enormous implications of population ageing, policies that reduce the vulnerability of older persons should be advanced with a view to producing gains not only for older persons and their families, but for the community, society at large and future generations as well.

333. Community-based targeting of social protection services can offer a promising means of delivering services to those in need, as the community becomes directly involved in identifying beneficiaries, thereby increasing accuracy in determining beneficiaries and promoting equity and inclusion by fostering greater local control over the programmes. Community-based targeting should be advanced in conjunction with the development of a politically sustainable social contract.

334. As mentioned above, the Poverty Reduction Strategy Paper process is being revisited in the light of the Millennium Development Goals and other commitments made at United Nations conferences and summits and their follow-up processes, with particular emphasis on promoting comprehensive measures that produce tangible benefits for poor people. In that context, more systematic consideration should be given to waiving user fees to ensure that poor people will have access to basic services such as primary education, preventive health care and clean water, or scholarships should be provided so that poor children can attend school.

VI. Rights-based approaches and rights deficit

335. Ascertaining and promoting the human rights of various social groups is increasingly being viewed as key to their empowerment and to reducing their vulnerabilities. Chapter VI reviews three attempts to develop a rights-based approach with respect to the advancement of indigenous peoples, migrants and persons with a disability.

Indigenous peoples

336. Rights-based approaches concerning indigenous peoples can be clustered around three broad policy areas: those pertaining to the land rights of indigenous peoples; those related to their cultural protection and promotion; and those mitigating the adverse impacts of current laws and socio-economic priorities of mainstream societies.

337. The transfer of land rights to indigenous peoples needs effective legal and judicial frameworks and action, including the fair enforcement of laws and the proper demarcation of territories. However, the typical approach to land transfers, involving land reform programmes in which parcels of land are transferred to individual peasants under the civil law of the mainstream society, runs counter to the communal rights philosophy governing indigenous cultures. Nonetheless, granting individual land rights entails a number of advantages, both economic and practical, from a mainstream point of view: the transfer already has a well-established legal basis; the individual title facilitates credit, as land can be used as collateral; and the practice encourages individual responsibility over the property. Since the title allows for the unrestricted disposal of the land, it provides flexibility for the owner and avoids the risk of condemning individuals to a single form of ownership.

338. The granting of land rights communally is usually favoured by indigenous peoples as being more consistent with their view of land use as communal or collective. It also provides flexibility on land use, thereby leading to better management of the environment and natural resources. The main disadvantage is that the land cannot be used as collateral and inhibits indigenous peoples' access to formal credit markets. Therefore, provisions for the communal transfer of land rights should also include special arrangements for credit access by indigenous peoples.

339. Whatever the means of transfer, it is critical to ensure that the process entails a proper and fair execution of laws. Too often, laws are simply not implemented, or their implementation is delayed through the judicial system. Those who can afford legal representation take advantage of legal loopholes or the loose interpretations of provisions. In addition, in the cases of unilateral abrogation of treaties between indigenous peoples and the States, indigenous peoples should have legal recourse within national or international law.

340. In recent years, awareness of the culture of indigenous peoples has increased and their culture has been given greater attention, nationally and internationally. Although the value of traditional medicines used by indigenous peoples is increasingly recognized, that knowledge has also led to concerns about piracy, as traditional knowledge is not protected by legal systems based on individual rights. Currently, indigenous rights to traditional medical knowledge and plants are being protected on a case-by-case basis in the courts. The issue that needs to be addressed is how collective traditional knowledge in the public domain can be protected from becoming part of the private and exclusive domain.

341. At the centre of the debate on promoting the wider use of traditional knowledge or preventing its misappropriation is the issue of how such knowledge can be effectively used to promote the development of indigenous peoples. Among indigenous peoples and environmental groups, there is opposition to the way patents are based on "discovery" without any invention, which exposes indigenous traditional knowledge to "discovery" by mainstream scientists. Among those groups, support is growing for a sui generis system that is based on "community", "collective" or "indigenous" rights to knowledge.

342. In this context, the World Trade Organization rules concerning Trade-Related Aspects of Intellectual Property Rights are perceived as restrictive to indigenous use of traditional knowledge, especially if patents and copyrights are based on or are similar to their traditional knowledge. Indigenous peoples are of the view that indigenous knowledge and cultural

heritage have evolved collectively and incrementally over generations. Consequently, no single person can claim invention or discovery of medicinal plants, seeds or other living things. It is therefore feared that the TRIPS agreement will lead to the appropriation of indigenous traditional medicinal plants and seeds as well as indigenous knowledge on health, agriculture and biodiversity conservation, eventually undermining traditional livelihoods.

343. A positive development is the support extended by the European Union to protect the genetic resources of indigenous peoples from exploitation by the biotechnology industry. The European Union proposals, to be discussed by the World Trade Organization, would require companies seeking patents to indicate the geographical origin of the natural products they are utilizing. The European Union also recommends that farmers be allowed to continue their traditional practice of saving and exchanging seeds, including those already patented.

344. States have the final responsibility for the resolution of indigenous land claims and cultural rights. Central to policies that accommodate the granting of indigenous rights are political and judicial systems and the frameworks for social and cultural justice specific to each State. It is necessary to consider the development objectives of both the State and the indigenous peoples, reconciling points of conflict. For such policies to succeed, they need to include laws protecting the rights of indigenous peoples and laws protecting them from institutional racism and discrimination.

345. ILO Convention No. 169, concerning Indigenous and Tribal Peoples in Independent Countries was adopted in 1989. It is the main international instrument dealing specifically with the human rights of indigenous peoples. Central to ILO Convention No. 169 is an approach based on respect for the specific identity of indigenous peoples and their right to participate in making decisions regarding their own destiny. However, the controversy surrounding the Convention has not abated over the years, and so far only 17 countries, of which 13 are in Latin America, have ratified it. Major differences exist concerning the absence of recognition of indigenous peoples' right to self-determination, since according to the Convention indigenous peoples would have only consultative status in policy decision-making and limited rights regarding lands and natural resources. As the Convention falls

short of their expectations, a number of indigenous peoples have called on Governments not to ratify it, and Government support is often lacking as well.

346. In this context, and in view of the repeated abuses of indigenous peoples' economic, social and cultural rights, several speakers before the second session of the Permanent Forum on Indigenous Issues, held in May 2003, stressed the importance of devising clear international guidelines on the human rights of indigenous populations. The Forum also called for the adoption, before the end of the International Decade of the World's Indigenous People (1995-2004), of the draft declaration on the rights of indigenous people. However, the fact that the draft declaration has been pending for nine years before the Commission on Human Rights serves as a reminder of the difficulty of the task ahead.

Migrants

347. Since the 1990s, many Governments have come to realize the discrepancy between the increasingly complex nature of current flows of migrants and the traditional institutional and legal frames of reference for immigration whereby each category of migrants is clearly and unequivocally identified. Such concerns have led to reassessments of international migration instruments. The existing international asylum regime defined by the 1951 Convention and its 1967 Protocol has been challenged by several Governments as no longer being relevant. Efforts by the International Labour Organization to obtain ratification of international conventions concerning migrant workers have been met with considerable opposition from a significant number of countries. Work done under the auspices of the United Nations Commission on Human Rights suggests that enforcement of migrants' human rights by national authorities has been inadequate in most parts of the world, while increasing manifestations of racism, xenophobia and other forms of discrimination and inhuman and degrading treatment against migrants have been reported.

348. The issue of discriminatory and sometimes abusive treatment of migrant workers has long been on the international agenda. Three principal instruments have been adopted that address that concern: ILO Convention No. 97 of 1949 concerning Migration for Employment; ILO Convention No. 143 of 1975 concerning Migration in Abusive Conditions and the

Promotion of Equality of Opportunity and Treatment of Migrant Workers; and the International Convention on the Protection of the Rights of All Migrant Workers and Members of Their Families of 1990.

349. Ratification of the Conventions is limited. As of July 2003, 42 countries had ratified ILO Convention No. 97, and 18 countries had ratified ILO Convention No. 143. The International Convention on Protection of the Rights of All Migrant Workers and Members of Their Families has been ratified by 22 countries and came into force on 1 July 2003. It is an important instrument in the broader struggle for the international protection of human rights. Few developed countries have become parties to the Conventions: 10 to ILO Convention No. 97; three to ILO Convention No. 143; and none to the 1990 Convention. In addition, the large majority of countries that have ratified ILO Convention No. 97 have excluded major provisions. Perhaps partly as a result of the limited ratification of the relevant international conventions, many States are employing a variety of cooperative approaches to migration management. Bilateral consultations and regional consultative processes in Europe, Africa, East Asia, South Asia and North and South America are addressing migration issues. In addition, the recent Berne Initiative[79] aims at sharing policy priorities and identifying long-term interests, common understandings and effective practices in the field of migration.

350. At the International Labour Conference of June 1999, ILO reviewed a study, based on communications with Governments, on the status of and prospects for its two conventions relating to migrant worker rights. The study clearly showed that while Governments seemed to agree on the broad terms of those instruments, they had clear reservations about specific provisions that pertained to the recruitment of migrant workers; social protection entitlements, which in certain cases might exceed entitlements under national legislations; rights afforded to migrants in an irregular situation; and, last and foremost, equality of opportunity and treatment between foreign workers and national workers. In addition, some of the conventions' provisions were considered outdated. For instance, those relating to equality of treatment between foreign workers and national workers no longer apply in the context of regional agreements on the freedom of movement and equality of treatment of nationals of member States of such entities as the European Union or MERCOSUR.

351. Nevertheless, there have been some positive developments. The appearance of the United Nations Guiding Principles on Internal Displacement (E/CN.4/1998/53/Add.2, annex) in 1998 was a milestone that for the first time set forth the rights of the internally displaced and the obligations of parties to conflicts with respect to the rights of those populations. In addition, in its resolution 55/25 of 15 November 2000, the General Assembly adopted the United Nations Convention against Transnational Organized Crime (Palermo Convention); the Protocol to Prevent, Suppress and Punish Trafficking in Persons, Especially Women and Children, supplementing the Convention; and the Protocol against the Smuggling of Migrants by Land, Sea and Air, also supplementing the Convention (General Assembly resolution 55/25, annexes I-III). The two protocols (Palermo Protocols) represent a significant international attempt to combat irregular migration and protect undocumented migrants' rights by emphasizing the criminal nature of smuggling.

352. The pattern of ratification of international conventions concerning migrant workers indicates the increasing reluctance of Governments to join such international instruments. It is too early to assess whether the Palermo Protocols will face the same fate. In the interim, the lack of basic agreement on a definition of migrant workers' rights has a serious bearing on the life of migrants and their families.

353. In the absence of specifically defined and internationally agreed migrant rights, international human rights instruments provide only for the legal protection of migrants. In addition, universal, regional and national human rights instruments embrace a large number of rights that have direct relevance to migrants. However, it is rights enforcement, rather than legal standards, that is the central issue.

354. Concerns with growing problems of mistreatment, discrimination and abuse of migrants reported by Governments of sending countries as well as by non-governmental organizations concerned with human rights led the United Nations Commission on Human Rights to appoint, in 1997, a Special Rapporteur on the human rights of migrants. The Commission also established the Working Group of intergovernmental experts on the human rights of

---

[79] Proposed by the Government of Switzerland at its international symposium on migration (June 2001).

migrants with the mandate to gather all relevant information on the obstacles existing to the effective and full protection of the human rights of migrants and to elaborate recommendations on strengthening the promotion, protection and implementation of the human rights of migrants.

355. A major finding of the Working Group is that in many parts of the world Governments are fully aware of a worsening trend in migrants' human rights, but that they seldom report taking measures to address the issue. Consequently, those who violate the human rights of migrants frequently end up doing so with impunity. The situation reveals that enforcing the human rights of migrants is not, in the eyes of public opinion or in the views of policy makers, as strong an obligation as that of enforcing the human rights of nationals.

356. To a significant extent, this state of affairs is a reflection of both prevailing anti-immigrant feelings and the lower legal and social status ascribed to migrants by host societies. Nevertheless, part of the explanation also lies in the fact that the violation of migrants' human rights often occurs where migrants are undocumented. Granting human rights to undocumented migrants is perceived by the public authority as undermining the rights of the State to enforce legality, a particularly important issue in contexts where stopping undocumented migration dominates government agendas.

Persons with disabilities

357. The development of disability rights approaches can be traced back to the 1970s. Two major declarations on the disabled were adopted by the General Assembly during that decade. The Declaration on the Rights of Mentally Retarded Persons (resolution 2856 (XXVI) of 20 December 1971) provided a framework for protecting rights through national and international action. The Declaration stated that mentally retarded persons had, to the degree feasible, the same rights as other human beings, including the right to proper medical care and education; to economic security; to a qualified guardian, as required; to protection from exploitation; and to due process of law and proper legal safeguards against every form of abuse. The Declaration stated that, if possible, mentally retarded persons should live with their families or with

foster parents and should participate in different forms of community life.

358. By its resolution 3447 (XXX) of 9 December 1975, the General Assembly adopted the Declaration on the Rights of Disabled Persons, which encouraged national and international protection of the rights of the disabled. The Declaration recognized that disabled persons were entitled to the same political and civil rights as others, including measures necessary to enable them to become self-sufficient. It proclaimed the rights of disabled persons, including the right to education; to medical treatment; and to placement services. It further recognized their rights to economic and social security; to employment; to live with their families; to participate in social and creative activities; to be protected against all exploitation and treatment of an abusive or degrading nature; and to avail themselves of qualified legal aid.

359. Both Declarations paved the way for future comprehensive sets of principles, which would eventually seek to integrate persons with disabilities into society, including the World Programme of Action concerning Disabled Persons (adopted by the General Assembly in its resolution 37/52 of 3 December 1982) and the Standard Rules on the Equalization of Opportunities for Persons with Disabilities (General Assembly resolution 48/96 of 20 December 1993, annex).

360. By promoting the prevention of disability, rehabilitation and the equalization of opportunities for persons with disabilities, the World Programme of Action represents an original synthesis of the movement towards a human rights model with more traditional disability concerns. While not abandoning the traditional efforts regarding disability (prevention and rehabilitation), the rights-based approach (equalization of opportunities) is clearly placed on an equal par with the more traditional concerns. The World Programme of Action recognizes the applicability of the Universal Declaration of Human Rights to persons with disabilities and provides concrete measures in the area of human rights.

361. The Standard Rules on the Equalization of Opportunities for Persons with Disabilities have made a major contribution to the emergence of international norms and standards relating to disability. The Rules, although not compulsory, offer persons with disabilities and their organizations an instrument for policy-

making and action while providing a basis for technical and economic cooperation. The Standard Rules include the Universal Declaration of Human Rights as part of their political and moral foundation. However, the Rules expand the human rights approach into areas not normally viewed as human rights concerns. Rule 2, for example, offers several provisions for States to ensure the provision of effective medical assistance to persons with disabilities.

362. In addition to the general normative and policy frameworks dealing with disability, two specific international instruments have been adopted: ILO Convention No. 159, and the Salamanca Statement and Framework for Action. ILO Convention No. 159 concerning "Vocational Rehabilitation and Employment (Disabled Persons) was adopted by the International Labour Conference in 1983 and since then has been ratified by some 73 countries. The purposes of the Convention are to ensure that appropriate vocational rehabilitation measures are made available to all categories of persons with disabilities and to promote employment opportunities for persons with disabilities in the labour market.

363. The Salamanca Statement on Principles, Policy and Practice in Special Needs Education, adopted at the World Conference on Special Needs Education organized by the United Nations Educational, Scientific and Cultural Organization (UNESCO) in cooperation with the Government of Spain in 1994, proclaimed that every child had a fundamental right to an education. Educational systems must take diversity into account, and those with special needs must have access to regular schools with an inclusive orientation. Governments were called upon to make the improvement of education a priority and adopt as a matter of law or policy the principle of inclusive education. The guiding principle was that schools should accommodate all children with a child-centred pedagogy.

364. The fact that the Standard Rules are not binding has raised significant concerns, and the question of a special convention on the rights of persons with disabilities has been actively discussed, initially by non-governmental organizations and more recently within the framework of an ad hoc committee of the General Assembly. While the question of a special convention has generated considerable interest, fundamental questions remain as to its scope and purpose as observed in the report of the Special

Rapporteur on Disability of the Commission for Social Development.[80] In his report, the Special Rapporteur identified the following basic questions: What areas should a future convention cover? What relation should it have to existing general conventions? Should it be expressed as a set of principles, general in nature but possible to apply in a variety of national situations around the world? Should the main perspective of the future convention be based on the needs in developing countries? Should this future convention replace the Standard Rules, or should the Standard Rules and the convention complement each other?

Recommendations

365. The special status attached to the language of human rights gives a universal moral authority to social claims that would otherwise rest on a value judgement. However, the cases analysed in the present chapter suggest that the force of law arises not so much from existing provisions that obligate the States, but from the social contract on which that law is based. In the absence of such social consensus, there seems to be little hope for enforcing existing entitlements, as evidenced by the reluctance of States to join, or to enforce, a very large number of binding international instruments dealing with economic, social and cultural rights. In fact, the connection between social development in general and the International Covenant on Economic, Social and Cultural Rights remains tenuous at best and non-existent at worst.

366. The legal status of indigenous peoples and the scope of jurisdiction accorded to States under treaties between the States and indigenous peoples should be clarified.

367. Innovative legal approaches are needed, at both the national and international levels, to address the issue of indigenous land rights, including how to incorporate indigenous peoples' communal ways of life into land rights solutions; to protect the culture of indigenous peoples; and to resolve the inconsistency between mainstream intellectual property rights and the traditional forms of collective ownership.

---

[80] See "Monitoring the implementation of the Standard Rules on the Equalization of Opportunities for Persons with Disabilities", a note by the Secretary-General (E/CN.5/2002/4), which contains the report of the Special Representative on his third mandate, 2000-2002.

368. The Agreement on Trade-Related Aspects of Intellectual Property Rights should be amended to better protect indigenous knowledge and resources.

369. New legal frames of reference for immigration should be developed, at both the national and international levels, that take into account the complex nature and dynamics of current flows of migrants. An international consensus should be sought on the basic rights of migrants. Enforcement of the basic rights of migrants should be moved to the top of the human rights agenda. International guidelines for the treatment of undocumented migrants should be developed.

370. The decision as to the scope and purpose of the proposed convention on the rights of persons with disabilities, particularly in respect of the relation between the convention and other general human rights instruments, should be informed by a realistic assessment of the contribution of those instruments to social development and the protection and empowerment of major social groups.

VII. Reduction of vulnerabilities, need for policy coherence and international cooperation

371. Success in meeting the objectives of development and poverty eradication depends to a significant extent on the creation of an enabling international economic environment and the adoption of effective measures, including new financial mechanisms, in order to support efforts by developing countries to achieve sustained economic growth and social and sustainable development and to strengthen their democratic systems. As a result, the focus of international cooperation has been primarily on the economic means, touching tangentially on the long-term social development objectives. Whereas international economic cooperation has a long history, international cooperation for social development remains at an early stage. Social development has largely been seen as a national task, supported by the international community mainly by means of aid, capacity-building and technical cooperation, and it is often contingent on such matters as good governance, democracy and the rule of law.

372. Globalization has put the existing framework for international cooperation to a test and has significantly increased awareness of the need for international cooperation for social development. Globalization has revealed a mismatch between existing national regulatory systems and institutions and the global nature of economic and financial operations within those systems and institutions, creating a new impetus for international cooperation and policy dialogue. In response to that challenge, a framework of economic and financial rules is being developed. However, no such framework or forum has been developed to address social issues, not even the social impacts of international economic decisions.

373. Furthermore, a major challenge to international cooperation for social development in developing countries is that development efforts are often reversed by violent upheavals and conflicts. The current high number and recurrence of such violent conflicts is a powerful reminder that conflict prevention is an integral part of the quest for social progress, development and the reduction of poverty.

374. Policy coherence and partnership, together with country ownership, have emerged as core organizing principles of today's international cooperation agenda

for development and have been abundantly discussed within the framework of the follow-up to the recent International Conference on Financing for Development, held in Monterrey, Mexico, and the Fourth Ministerial Conference of the World Trade Organization, held in Doha. However, those processes have focused largely on increasing the coherence of economic policies through more effective coordination and cooperation at the national, regional and global levels. They have paid little attention to the interdependence between social and economic policies or to the promotion of holistic, integrated, comprehensive and consistent public policies.

375. This state of affairs is a direct consequence of the dominant macroeconomic policy perspective, which posits that social development will naturally follow economic growth. Consequently, issues of distribution and social development objectives are not explicitly addressed, nor is any significant attention paid to assessing and understanding the social consequences of economic policies. However, almost 10 years after the World Summit for Social Development, it has become clear that, although sustained and pro-poor economic growth is undoubtedly critical to poverty reduction, other fundamental instruments of development such as employment and social integration need to be forcefully reintroduced as elements of policy if the causes of social vulnerabilities, and not only the symptoms of poverty, are to be successfully addressed.

376. Political commitment, however, is unlikely to translate into policy efficiency in the absence, as is presently the case, of innovative conceptual and operational frameworks that would ensure coherence between economic and social policies. The full scope of interdependence between economic and social development remains largely uncharted, and the policy implications of that interdependence are rarely addressed. As mentioned previously, there is still insufficient coordination in the Poverty Reduction Strategy Papers between policies to promote the social inclusion of the poorest and most marginalized groups, on the one hand, and development, on the other hand.

377. Much hope has been placed on recent initiatives that attempt to develop innovative ways of combining social and economic objectives, including the Global

Employment Agenda, the Youth Employment Network, the World Commission on the Social Dimension of Globalization and the New Partnership for Africa's Development (NEPAD). The initiatives are a step towards the establishment of an operational partnership for social development, in particular through the sharing of experiences and practices, and should serve as the basis for expanding international cooperation for social development, with the overall objective of strengthening governance and achieving policy coherence at all levels, from local to global.

378. In the absence of conceptual and operational frameworks that would ensure coherence between economic and social policies, the main short-term objective for international cooperation in the reduction of social vulnerabilities is to advance and operationalize the specific agendas for empowerment and participation put forward by the different social groups. A concrete way to achieve this would be to systematically mainstream those agendas into frameworks that aim at improving coordination among development partners and cohesiveness among programmes and policies, such as the United Nations Development Assistance Framework and the Common Country Assessment, also prepared by the United Nations, as well as the United Nations Development Programme Country Cooperation Framework and the Poverty Reduction Strategy Papers.

379. The lack of coherence in development policies and international cooperation is startling. For example, during the discussions that have taken place since the Second World Assembly on Ageing, it has become clear that, in their development strategies, both development institutions and national Governments have largely overlooked the impact of a growing older population and changes in intergenerational relations. International development targets and the Millennium Development Goals, for example, set targets that spotlight women and children in the areas of poverty eradication, education and health, but older generations are a critical omission in relevant discussions on the development process. To some extent, issues related to ageing were included in the International Conference on Financing for Development and the World Summit on Sustainable Development. Nonetheless, although issues related to ageing and older persons are gradually being addressed within the framework of the various global processes, they are still far from gaining the attention called for in the Madrid Plan of Action on Ageing.

380. Awareness of the need to develop comprehensive development strategies for other social groups, including indigenous peoples and persons with disabilities, has increased, as exemplified by such initiatives as the Permanent Forum on Indigenous Issues and the current development of a comprehensive and integral international convention to promote and protect the rights and dignity of persons with disabilities. However, further efforts are still needed to address the lack of coherence in development policies and international cooperation. Certainly, the inclusion of all population groups, including older persons, within the context of globalization is one of the keys to realizing the Millennium Development Goals and reducing social vulnerabilities.

Recommendations

381. The basis for social vulnerability, as it is defined in the context of the present report, is economic insecurity. Thus, economic growth and employment creation should be given due consideration in the policy steps taken to reduce social vulnerability, reflecting the emphasis placed on poverty reduction in the Millennium Declaration. However, experience has shown that the trickle-down effect of economic growth per se cannot be relied upon to remedy social problems.

382. Social vulnerability is a complex phenomenon with its causes rooted in social, economic and cultural institutions and practices. As a result, approaches to policy aimed at reducing social vulnerability must be multi-pronged and internally consistent: an integration of social and economic policy is a necessity to alleviate the impact of vulnerabilities on affected individuals, households, communities and social groups. However, that does not imply that policy measures have to be implemented simultaneously or that prioritization is impossible. Quite to the contrary, focus and priorities are necessary for policy to be effective, especially in today's general environment of limited public sector resources. To maximize the effectiveness of policy responses, policy makers need to take an integrated approach to the problem while keeping the appropriate priorities. This approach requires an understanding of the complex relationships between the various dimensions and causes of social vulnerability and the

development of new and effective ways to coordinate the delivery of economic and social policies.

383. Although sound economic policy is essential, enhancement of the capacity of excluded groups to make demands on service provision and effect policy change is of paramount importance to the reduction of social vulnerabilities, as is assertive public intervention to promote social cohesion.

384. Furthermore, institutional capacity-building and the development of some form of social protection are important steps for developing countries to take to deal with the consequences of modernization and globalization. In developed countries, reforms of the pension system and other programmes of social protection also need to take into account the changes that are occurring with regard to population ageing, the family and the increased movement of goods, capital and people among countries. Finally, better targeted, informed and participative policies are also necessary in addressing specific dimensions of social vulnerability.

Conclusion

385. Well over a billion people in our world today are living without enough food to eat, without safe water to drink and without primary schooling or health care for their children — in short, without the most basic elements required for human dignity. The social groups considered in the *Report on the World Social Situation, 2003,* are not only included in that group but are often among the poorest of them. Lack of income, social ills, social and cultural biases and discrimination are part and parcel of their daily lives.

386. Almost 10 years ago, at the World Summit for Social Development, the point was made that a stable economy cannot be built in an unstable society and that without stable social underpinnings, it would be difficult for economic development to be sustainable.

387. The degree, pervasiveness and persistence of social vulnerability in all parts of the world show that such stability is still far from becoming a reality. Nonetheless, it would appear that economic policies are being pursued without giving much thought to the underlying social conditions, or, at best, they are being pursued with the notion that their achievement will take care of social ills and instability.

388. Nevertheless, without economic stability, especially macroeconomic stability, it will be difficult to attack the sources of vulnerability and, by extension, the causes of poverty. This is the case not only because such stability is important for economic growth but also because macroeconomic stability makes it possible for policy makers to look beyond the short term. In a stable environment, policy makers will be able to turn their attention to long-term structural issues, not the least of which is inequity — and equity is the basic ingredient for having a stable society.

389. Macroeconomic policies, however, are essentially only a means to an end and not an end in themselves. In his report to the fortieth session of the Commission for Social Development on the integration of social and economic policy, the Secretary-General stated, "... the ultimate ends of economic policy are in the broadest sense 'social'" (E/CN.5/2002/3, para. 5). Therefore, it is essential for explicit social objectives to be included in macroeconomic policy-making. They should be included, not as an afterthought or something that will come to pass once the macroeconomic variables are behaving correctly, but as a direct combination of economic and social policies.

390. When surveying the terrain of social vulnerability and the social groups that suffer from it, one is hard pressed to find such a direct combination. The conditions social groups and individuals face are not easily addressed or overcome by policies that deal with macro-aggregates. The particulars and peculiarities of social groups require a much more fine-tuned approach. A complex policy mix is necessary rather than such "blunt" instruments as fiscal, monetary and exchange-rate policies, open trading and financial systems, if the dire situation in which the social groups find themselves is to be overcome.

391. Unfortunately, there is little evidence that such policies are forthcoming. Not only are they more difficult to design and implement but they also concern the future welfare of those whose plight can most easily be ignored, who are largely powerless and voiceless.

392. In his Nobel Lecture upon receiving the Nobel Peace Prize, the Secretary-General stated:

"No one today is unaware of [the] divide between the world's rich and poor. No one today can claim ignorance of the cost that this divide imposes on the poor and dispossessed who are no less deserving of human dignity, fundamental freedoms, security, food and education than any of us. The costs, however, are not borne by them alone. Ultimately it is borne by all of us — North and South, rich and poor, men and women of all races and religions."[81]

393. While it is no longer possible to claim ignorance, it is still all too easy to turn a blind eye to those who live on the wrong side of the divide. Societies perpetuate this stance at their peril. Overcoming social vulnerability and eradicating poverty are global responsibilities. They are obligations based not only on self-interest but also on solidarity and social justice rooted in the notions of common humanity, common destiny and the pursuit of the common good. Those are the ideals upon which the United Nations is founded, and they represent the spirit in which the *Report* is written.

---

[81] United Nations press release (SG/SM/8071). Also available from http://www.nobel.se/peace/laureates/2001/annan-lecture.html.

Annex tables

Table A.1
Assessing vulnerabilities: income poverty

	International poverty line	
Country	Survey year	Population living on less than $1 a day (Percentage)
Algeria	1995	<2
Armenia	1998	13
Azerbaijan	2001	4
Bangladesh	2000	36
Belarus	2000	<2
Bolivia	1999	14
Botswana	1993	24
Brazil	1998	10
Bulgaria	2001	5
Burkina Faso	1994	61
Burundi	1998	58
Cameroon	1996	33
Central African Republic	1993	67
Chile	1998	<2
China	2000	16
Colombia	1998	14
Costa Rica	1998	7
Côte d'Ivoire	1995	12
Croatia	2000	<2
Czech Republic	1996	<2
Dominican Republic	1998	<2
Ecuador	1995	20
Egypt	2000	3
El Salvador	1997	21
Estonia	1998	<2
Ethiopia	1999-2000	82
Gambia	1998	59
Georgia	1998	<2
Ghana	1999	45
Guatemala	2000	16
Guyana	1998	<2
Honduras	1998	24
Hungary	1998	<2

Country	International poverty line	
	Survey year	Population living on less than $1 a day (Percentage)
India	1999-2000	35
Indonesia	2000	7
Iran (Islamic Republic of)	1998	<2
Jamaica	2000	<2
Jordan	1997	<2
Kazakhstan	1996	1.5
Kenya	1997	23
Kyrgyzstan	2000	2
Lao People's Democratic Republic	1997-1998	26
Latvia	1998	<2
Lesotho	1993	43
Lithuania	2000	<2
Madagascar	1999	49
Malawi	1997-1998	42
Malaysia	1997	<2
Mali	1994	73
Mauritania	1995	29
Mexico	1998	8
Mongolia	1995	14
Morocco	1999	<2
Mozambique	1996	38
Namibia	1993	35
Nepal	1995	38
Nicaragua	1998	82
Niger	1995	61
Nigeria	1997	70
Pakistan	1998	13
Panama	1998	8
Paraguay	1998	20
Peru	1996	16
Philippines	2000	15
Poland	1998	<2
Portugal	1994	<2
Republic of Korea	1998	<2
Republic of Moldova	2001	22
Romania	2000	2
Russian Federation	2000	6
Rwanda	1983-1985	36

Country	International poverty line	
	Survey year	Population living on less than $1 a day (Percentage)
Senegal	1995	26
Sierra Leone	1989	57
Slovakia	1996	<2
Slovenia	1998	<2
South Africa	1995	<2
Sri Lanka	1995-1996	7
Tajikistan	1998	10
Thailand	2000	<2
The former Yugoslav Republic of Macedonia	1998	<2
Trinidad and Tobago	1992	12
Tunisia	1995	<2
Turkey	2000	<2
Turkmenistan	1998	12
Uganda	1996	82
Ukraine	1999	3
United Republic of Tanzania	1993	20
Uruguay	1998	<2
Uzbekistan	1998	19
Venezuela	1998	15
Viet Nam	1998	18
Yemen	1998	16
Zambia	1998	64
Zimbabwe	1990-1991	36

Source: World Bank, *World Development Indicators*, *2003* (Washington, D.C., 2003).

Table A.2
Assessing vulnerabilities: unemployment, urban informal sector employment and pension contributions

Country	Unemployment[a] (Percentage)			Urban informal sector employment[b] (Percentage)			Pension contribution[c]
	Unemployed male labour force	Unemployed female labour force	Unemployed labour force	Males in urban informal sector employment	Females in urban informal sector employment	Total population in urban informal sector employment	Contributors among total informal working-age population (Percentage)
Albania	16	21	18				31
Algeria	12	14	13				23
Argentina				48	36	43	39
Armenia	5	15	9				49
Australia	7	7	6				
Austria	5	5	5				77
Azerbaijan	1	1	1				46
Bangladesh							3
Belarus	6	9	2				94
Belgium	7	12	7				66
Bolivia				12		53	13
Botswana					28	19	
Brazil	7	14	10	43	31	38	31
Bulgaria	14	14	14				63
Burkina Faso							3
Burundi							3
Cameroon							12
Canada	7	7	7				80
Chad							1
Chile	9	10	10	33	32	32	35
China	5	4	3				17
China, Hong Kong SAR	5		5				
Colombia	17	25	21	49	44	47	29
Costa Rica	5	8	6	43	36	40	39
Côte d'Ivoire				37	73	53	9
Croatia	13	15	21	6	7	6	57
Czech Republic	7	11	9				67

Country	Unemployment[a] (Percentage)			Urban informal sector employment[b] (Percentage)			Pension contribution[c]
	Unemployed male labour force	Unemployed female labour force	Unemployed labour force	Males in urban informal sector employment	Females in urban informal sector employment	Total population in urban informal sector employment	Contributors among working-age population (Percentage)
Democratic Republic of the Congo							6
Denmark	5	6	5				88
Dominican Republic	8	25	14				18
Ecuador	8	16	12	54	55	53	34
Egypt	5	20	8				34
El Salvador	8	6	7				25
Estonia	13	10	15				67
Ethiopia				19	53	33	
Finland	10	11	10				84
France	9	12	10				75
Gabon							14
Gambia	15	12	14				
Georgia							40
Germany	8	9	8				82
Ghana			79				9
Greece	7	17	11				73
Guatemala							19
Guinea							2
Honduras	4	4	4	53	58	55	18
Hungary	8	6	7				65
India							8
Indonesia			6	19	23	21	7
Iran (Islamic Republic of)				3	90	18	25
Ireland	5	5	5				65
Israel	9	8	8				63
Italy	9	16	11				68
Jamaica	10	23	16	26	21	24	46
Japan	5	5	5				92

Country	Unemployment[a] (Percentage)			Urban informal sector employment[b] (Percentage)			Pension contribution[c]
	Unemployed male labour force	Unemployed female labour force	Unemployed labour force	Males in urban informal sector employment	Females in urban informal sector employment	Total population in urban informal sector employment	Contributors among urban informal working-age population (Percentage)
Jordan	12	21	13				25
Kazakhstan			14			12	28
Kenya						58	24
Kyrgyzstan						12	42
Latvia	16	13	8			17	52
Lithuania	20	14	17	12	5	9	
Madagascar							5
Malaysia			3			58	38
Mali						71	2
Mauritania							4
Mauritius							57
Mexico	2	3	2	38	30	35	31
Mongolia	5	6	6				
Morocco	20	28	22				11
Mozambique							2
Myanmar				53	57	54	
Nepal	2	1	1				75
Netherlands	3	5	4				
New Zealand	6	6	6				
Nicaragua	9	15	13				13
Niger							2
Nigeria							1
Norway	4	3	3				86
Pakistan	4	15	6				2
Panama	11	18	13	36	28	32	41
Paraguay				45	53	58	9
Peru	8	9	8			48	25
Philippines	10	11	10	16	19	17	14
Poland	15	19	17	14	11	13	64

Country	Unemployment[a] (Percentage)			Urban informal sector employment[b] (Percentage)			Pension contribution[c]
	Unemployed male labour force	Unemployed female labour force	Unemployed labour force	Males in urban informal sector employment	Females in urban informal sector employment	Total population in urban informal sector employment	Contributors among urban working-age population (Percentage)
Portugal	3	5	4				80
Puerto Rico	12	8	10				
Republic of Korea	7	5	4				43
Republic of Moldova			11				
Romania	7	6	11				48
Russian Federation	14	13	11				13
Rwanda							13
Senegal							5
Singapore	5	5	4				56
Slovakia	16	16	19	25	11	19	72
Slovenia	8	7	8				69
South Africa	20	28	23	11	26	17	
Spain	10	21	14				61
Sri Lanka	7	16	11				21
Sudan							12
Sweden	7	7	5				89
Switzerland	2	3	3				97
Thailand	3	3	2	75	79	77	17
The former Yugoslav Republic of Macedonia	33	38	35				47
Togo	11	17	13				15
Trinidad and Tobago							
Tunisia	8	7	9				23
Turkey							27
Ukraine	12	12	12	5	5	5	66
United Kingdom	7	5	5				85
United Republic of Tanzania				60	85	67	2
United States	4	5	4				92
Uruguay	9	15	11	39	41	36	78

77

Country	Unemployment[a] (Percentage)			Urban informal sector employment[b] (Percentage)			Pension contribution[c]
	Unemployed male labour force	Unemployed female labour force	Unemployed labour force	Males in urban informal sector employment	Females in urban informal sector employment	Total population in urban informal sector employment	Contributors among informal working-age population (Percentage)
Venezuela			15	47			18
Viet Nam					46	47	10
West Bank and Gaza Strip			14				
Zambia							8
Zimbabwe	7	5	6				10

Source: World Bank, *World Development Indicators 2003* (Washington, D.C., 2003).

[a] Unemployment figures are measured from 1998-2001.
[b] Urban employment figures are measured from 1995-1999.
[c] Pension contributions figures are from 1990-2001, depending on the country.

Table A.3

Assessing vulnerabilities among children and youth: poor health, exploitation in the labour market and illiteracy

Country	Child malnutrition: children under the age of five[a] (Percentage)		Children of age group 10-14 in the labour force (Percentage)		Youth illiteracy rates[b]	
	Weight for age	Height for age	1980	2001	Percentage of males aged 15-24	Percentage of females aged 15-24
Afghanistan	49	48	28	24		
Albania	14	15			1	3
Algeria	6	18			6	15
Angola	41	53	30	26		
Argentina	5	12	8	2	2	1
Armenia	3	13				
Australia	0	0				
Azerbaijan	17	20				
Bangladesh	48	45	35	27	43	60
Benin	23	31	30	26	28	63
Bolivia	8	27	19	11	2	6
Bosnia and Herzegovina	4					
Botswana	13	29	26	14	15	8
Brazil	6	11	19	14	6	3
Burkina Faso	34	37	71	42	53	75
Burundi	45		50	48	33	36
Cambodia	45	45	27	24	16	25
Cameroon	22	29	34	23	8	11
Central African Republic	23	28			23	39
Chad	28	29	42	36	25	38
Chile	1	2			1	1
China	10	14	30	7	1	3
China, Hong Kong SAR					1	
Colombia	7	14	12	6	4	2
Congo			27	25	2	3
Costa Rica	5	6	10	4	2	1
Côte d'Ivoire	21	25	28	18	29	46
Croatia	1	1				
Democratic Republic of the Congo	34	45	33	28	11	24
Democratic Republic of Korea	28					
Dominican Republic	5	11	25	13	9	8
Ecuador	14	26	9	4	2	3
Egypt	4	19	18	9	23	36

Country	Child malnutrition: children under the age of five[a] (Percentage)		Children of age group 10-14 in the labour force (Percentage)		Youth illiteracy rates[b]	
	Weight for age	Height for age	1980	2001	Percentage of males aged 15-24	Percentage of females aged 15-24
El Salvador	12	23	17	13	11	12
Eritrea	44	38	44	38	19	39
Ethiopia	47	52	46	41	38	50
Gabon	12	21	29	13		
Gambia	17	30	44	33	33	49
Georgia	3	12				
Ghana	25	26	16	12	6	11
Guatemala	24	46	19	14	14	27
Guinea	33	41	41	31		
Guinea-Bissau	25		43	36	26	54
Haiti	17	23	33	22	35	34
Honduras	17	39	14	7	16	13
India	53	52	21	12	20	34
Indonesia	25	42	13	7	2	3
Iran (Islamic Republic of)	11	15	14	2	4	8
Iraq			11	2	40	70
Israel						1
Jamaica	4	4			9	2
Jordan	5	8			1	1
Kazakhstan	4	10				
Kenya	22	33	45	39	4	5
Kuwait	2	3			8	6
Kyrgyzstan	11	25				
Lao People's Democratic Republic	40	41	31	25	15	28
Lebanon	3	12			3	7
Lesotho	18	44	28	20	17	1
Liberia			26	15	14	46
Libyan Arab Jamahiriya	5	15				6
Madagascar	40	48	40	34	16	23
Malawi	25	49	45	31	19	38
Malaysia	20		8	2	2	2
Mali	27	49	61	50	52	74
Mauritania	32	35	30	22	43	59
Mauritius	15	10	5	2	6	5
Mexico	8	18	9	5	2	3
Mongolia	13	25	4	1	1	1

Country	Child malnutrition: children under the age of five[a] (Percentage)		Children of age group 10-14 in the labour force (Percentage)		Youth illiteracy rates[b]	
	Weight for age	Height for age	1980	2001	Percentage of males aged 15-24	Percentage of females aged 15-24
Morocco			21	1	23	40
Mozambique	26	36	39	32	24	52
Myanmar	43	45	28	23	9	9
Namibia			34	17	10	6
Nepal	48	51	56	41	23	56
Nicaragua	12	25	19	12	29	27
Niger	40	40	48	43	67	86
Nigeria	31	34	29	24	10	15
Oman	23	23				3
Pakistan	38	36	23	15	38	57
Panama	8	18	6	2	3	4
Papua New Guinea			28	17	20	28
Paraguay			15	5	3	3
Peru	7	25	4	2	2	5
Philippines	32	32	14	5	1	1
Portugal			8	1		
Puerto Rico					3	2
Russian Federation	3	13				
Rwanda	24	43	43	41	14	17
Saudi Arabia					5	9
Senegal	18	23	43	26	40	57
Sierra Leone	27		19	14		
Somalia	26	23	38	31		
South Africa	9	23			8	9
Sri Lanka	33	20	4	2	3	3
Sudan	11	34	33	27	17	27
Swaziland	10		17	12	10	8
Syrian Arab Republic	13	21	14	2	4	20
Tajikistan		31				
Thailand	18	13	25	11	1	2
The Former Yugoslav Republic of Macedonia	6	7				
Togo	25	22	36	27	12	35
Tunisia	4	8			2	10
Turkey	8	16	21	7	1	6
Turkmenistan	12	22				

Country	Child malnutrition: children under the age of five[a] (Percentage)		Children of age group 10-14 in the labour force (Percentage)		Youth illiteracy rates[b]	
	Weight for age	Height for age	1980	2001	Percentage of males aged 15-24	Percentage of females aged 15-24
Uganda	23	39	49	43	14	27
Ukraine	3	16				
United Arab Emirates	7				12	5
United Republic of Tanzania	29	44	43	36	6	11
United States	1	2				
Uruguay	4	10	4	1	1	1
Uzbekistan	19	31				
Venezuela	4	13			3	1
Viet Nam	34	37	22	5	5	4
West Bank and Gaza Strip	15					
Yemen	46	52	26	18	16	51
Yugoslavia[c]	2	5				
Zambia	24	42	19	15	9	14
Zimbabwe	13	27	37	27	1	4
Region						
East Asia and Pacific			27	8	2	4
Europe and Central Asia	15	14	3	1		1
Latin America and Caribbean			13	8	5	5
Middle East and North Africa	9	19	14	4	14	26
South Asia	15		23	15	24	41
Sub-Saharan Africa	53	47	35	29	18	27

Source: World Bank, *World Development Indicators, 2003* (Washington, D.C., 2003).

[a] Prevalence of child malnutrition: percentage of children under the age of five measured from 1993-2001.
[b] Figures for youth illiteracy rates are from 2001.
[c] As of 4 February 2003, the official name of "Yugoslavia" has been changed to "Serbia and Montenegro".

03-42620 (E)   300903

كيفية الحصول على منشورات الأمم المتحدة

يمكن الحصول على منشورات الأمم المتحدة من المكتبات ودور التوزيع في جميع أنحاء العالم . استعلم عنها من المكتبة
التي تتعامل معها أو اكتب إلى : الأمم المتحدة ، قسم البيع في نيويورك أو في جنيف .

如何购取联合国出版物

联合国出版物在全世界各地的书店和经售处均有发售。请向书店询问或写信到纽约或日内瓦的
联合国销售组。

HOW TO OBTAIN UNITED NATIONS PUBLICATIONS

United Nations publications may be obtained from bookstores and distributors throughout the
world. Consult your bookstore or write to: United Nations, Sales Section, New York or Geneva.

COMMENT SE PROCURER LES PUBLICATIONS DES NATIONS UNIES

Les publications des Nations Unies sont en vente dans les librairies et les agences dépositaires
du monde entier. Informez-vous auprès de votre libraire ou adressez-vous à : Nations Unies,
Section des ventes, New York ou Genève.

КАК ПОЛУЧИТЬ ИЗДАНИЯ ОРГАНИЗАЦИИ ОБЪЕДИНЕННЫХ НАЦИЙ

Издания Организации Объединенных Наций можно купить в книжных магазинах
и агентствах во всех районах мира. Наводите справки об изданиях в вашем книжном
магазине или пишите по адресу: Организация Объединенных Наций, Секция по
продаже изданий, Нью-Йорк или Женева.

COMO CONSEGUIR PUBLICACIONES DE LAS NACIONES UNIDAS

Las publicaciones de las Naciones Unidas están en venta en librerías y casas distribuidoras en
todas partes del mundo. Consulte a su librero o diríjase a: Naciones Unidas, Sección de Ventas,
Nueva York o Ginebra.